# 101 HANGOVER RECIPES

**PAGE 105**
**ULTIMATE RESTAURANT BURGER**
with bacon, cheese, and tomato relish

# 101 HANGOVER RECIPES

### BEAT THE BOOZE WITH THESE TASTY RECIPES FOR MORNING-AFTER MUNCHIES

COMPILED BY
## Dan Vaux-Nobes

DOG 'n' BONE

First published in the United Kingdom
in 2015 by Ryland Peters & Small
20–21 Jockey's Fields
London WC1R 4BW

341 E 116th St
New York, NY 10029

www.ry'

10 9 8 [7] 6 5 4 3 2 1

Recipe [...] Ballard, Jordan Bourke, Mickael Benichou,
Vatchai [...] Bhumichitr, Susannah Blake, Dominic Bliss, Celia Brooks
Brown, [...] [Maxwell] Clark, Linda Collister, Ross Dobson,
Dr Hasl [...]
Harkins [...] Katie Ellis, Clare Ferguson, Manisha Gambhir
Kate Ha [...] Elsa Petersen [...] Louise Pickford
May, Ha [...]
Reed, A [...] Linda Stevenson,
Fran Wa [...] Laura Washburn, Ryland, Peters &
Small, a [...] nd Dog 'n' Bone Books 201[...]

Recipe [...] © Dog 'n' Bone Books 2016

Design and photography © Dog 'n' Bone Books 2016

A CIP catalog record for this book is available from the Library of
Congress and the British Library.

ISBN: 978 1 909313 90 3

Printed in China

Design concept: Eoghan O'Brien
Designer: Jerry Goldie
Commissioning editor: Pete Jorgensen
Art director: Sally Powell
Production controller: Sarah Kulasek-Boyd
Publishing manager: Penny Craig
Publisher: Cindy Richards
Picture credits: See page 144

# CONTENTS

# INTRODUCTION

HANGOVERS ARE THE WORST. IN FACT, THE ONLY THING MORE ANNOYING THAN A HANGOVER IS THE PERSON YOU KNOW WHO ALWAYS SAYS, "I NEVER GET HANGOVERS." LUCKY/LYING BASTARD. STILL, IF YOU'RE GOING TO EXPERIENCE THE SWEET, SWEET HIGH OF GETTING HAMMERED WITH YOUR FRIENDS YOU WILL RUN THE RISK OF GOING HEAD-TO-HEAD WITH THAT MORTAL ENEMY OF ALL BOOZERS: THE HANGOVER, ALONG WITH ITS HATEFUL SIDEKICKS, HEADACHE AND NAUSEA.

So what do you do when you finally wake up in your pit after the bender to end all benders and tentatively move your head out from under the covers, only to realize that any additional movement is going to either a) make you chuck your guts up, or b) cause a pain in your skull that's equivalent to someone tattooing a picture of your pitifully hungover face directly onto your eyeballs? Well, you either sob pathetically, or you try and do something about it by getting some food into that delicate stomach to soak up the booze you swilled last night.

Everyone's different when it comes to hangover munch, which is why this book contains over 100 recipes to help you on the road to recovery. Some of you will be the masochistic sort who like to hit the gym in an effort to sweat out some of the booze and say sorry to your body for the punishment you put it through the previous evening. For these people there are two chapters of disgustingly wholesome recipes—Juices, Smoothies, and Shakes and Healthy and (Pseudo) Scientific Meals, which contain various superfoods and other immune-system bolstering ingredients to help end your hangover torture.

For the more normal drinkers—aka the lazy bastards—who prefer to spend hungover Sundays sat in their boxers watching repeats of *Friends*, there's a chapter on Quick

Fixes that features recipes involving little more than chopping up a few ingredients and switching on a toaster. Balls-to-the-wall boozers will appreciate some of the restorative drinks in the Hair of the Dog Cocktails section, and anyone with a sweet tooth will find something to suit in the tooth-achingly sweet Sugar Bombs chapter. Throughout, the pages are also peppered with liberal helpings of bacon—the essential lifesaving, restorative ingredient that has done more to stop hangovers than any alcohol advisory board ever could.

Finally, there are dishes for those of you with either minor hangovers or a bit more ambition when it comes to the food stakes. It's completely understandable that you're not going to want to cook a roast dinner if you're suffering from the kind of hangover that renders you completely incapable of doing anything other than sobbing quietly to yourself as you reach yet again for the sick bucket. But

if you are the type of hanging person who's happy to spend some time in front of the stove in order to create the perfect recovery meal then well done, you are one of life's good guys, a gold star in human hangover form. Not only does your get-up-and-go attitude mark you out for big things, but your lazy partner/housemates/friends will also thank their lucky stars that they met someone prepared to feed them delicious meals during times of desperate need. Or you could just make them promise to do all your household chores for the next month/pay for your next night out/give you extortionate amounts of cash in return for one of the dishes in the Hunger Busters or Carb Loading chapters.

One last piece of advice: a bit of planning is important when it comes to hangover cooking. Some of the recipes

contain a few ingredients that you might not have lying around. Don't be that idiot who attempts to drag him/herself, *Day-of-the-Dead*-like, down to the nearest convenience store to procure some fresh herbs, only to come back broken and dejected having discovered the only "food" sold there is instant noodles and canned bacon. Instead, have a flick through these pages the morning before a big night out, plan what you're going to cook, and get the ingredients while you're still in a reasonable state. That way the furthest you'll have to drag your hungover ass is into the kitchen.

# CHAPTER 1

# JUICES, SMOOTHIES, AND SHAKES

## GREEN DAY

DESPITE FEELING ABSOLUTELY HANGING, IF YOU CAN MANAGE TO NECK THIS UNDOUBTEDLY HEALTHY, LURID GREEN CONCOCTION, YOUR ABUSED LIVER WILL GET A BOOST OF AN ENZYME CALLED GLUTATHIONE, WHICH HELPS TO CLEANSE IT OF HEAVY METALS. BRASSICAS SUCH AS BROCCOLI, CABBAGE, AND KALE CONTAIN THE NUTRIENTS DOING THE BOOSTING, SO IF YOU CAN FACE IT, FEEL FREE TO SUBSTITUTE THE BROCCOLI FOR SOMETHING EQUALLY DISGUSTINGLY HEALTHY.

★ Put the apple, broccoli, arugula (rocket), cucumber, lemon juice, coconut water, and wheatgrass powder in a blender, and blend until smooth.

★ Add a splash of water if too thick. Divide between 2 glasses and serve.

1 green apple, quartered, cored, and cut into wedges

4 broccoli florets

a handful of arugula (rocket) leaves

½ cucumber, peeled, deseeded, and cut into chunks

freshly squeezed juice of ½ lemon

1 cup (250 ml) coconut water

1–2 teaspoons wheatgrass powder

a splash of pure or filtered water (optional)

**serves 2**

# MORNING CLEANSER

SADLY, DESPITE THE RATHER PROMISING NAME, THIS JUICE WON'T CLEANSE ANY SHAMEFUL DRUNKEN MEMORIES FROM THE NIGHT BEFORE. BUT IT DOES THE NEXT BEST THING... THAT'S RIGHT, IT SOOTHES YOUR INNARDS WITH PEARS AND PROMOTES URINE PRODUCTION WITH CUCUMBER—THE BEST DIURETIC AROUND! FINALLY, AND MOST IMPORTANTLY, IT AIDS YOUR BODY IN OVERCOMING ALCOHOL INTOXICATION DUE TO THE GRAPEFRUIT. WINNER!

4 firm ripe pears, about 1 lb. 7 oz. (650 g)

½ cucumber

1 small grapefruit

2-in. (5-cm) piece fresh ginger

**serves 2**

★ Cut the pears and cucumber into chunks. Peel the grapefruit and cut into wedges. Press everything through a juicer into a pitcher (jug).

# ROCKET FUEL

NOW WE'RE TALKING! IF YOU'RE AN ADVOCATE OF THE "KILL IT WITH FIRE" SCHOOL OF HANGOVER RECOVERY, THIS ONE'S FOR YOU. THERE ARE LOADS OF NUTRIENTS IN THIS JUICE, BUT IT'S THE CHILI THAT WILL GIVE YOU THAT "GET UP AND GET ON WITH IT" SCORCHING JOLT.

2 apples, quartered, cored, and cut into wedges

2 large handfuls of curly kale

1 handful of broccoli, both florets and stalks, chopped

2 carrots, peeled and halved lengthwise

2 handfuls of alfalfa sprouts

1 red chili, quartered lengthwise

2 teaspoons freshly squeezed lemon juice

1–2 teaspoons powdered greens or barleygrass powder

**serves 2**

★ Juice the apples, kale, broccoli, carrots, alfalfa sprouts, and three-quarters of the chili. Stir in the lemon juice and powdered greens or barleygrass. Divide between 2 glasses.

★ Finely chop the reserved chili and sprinkle over each glass.

# FROZEN FRUIT JUICE GRANITAS

MAYBE YOU'VE WOKEN UP WITH A HANGOVER THAT'S LEFT YOU WITH A MOUTH DRIER THAN DEATH VALLEY, OR PERHAPS YOU'VE OVERDONE IT ON THE CHILIS IN THE AFOREMENTIONED "ROCKET FUEL" (SEE PAGE 9)? IN EITHER CASE, THIS ONE'S FOR YOU. PROBABLY BEST TO PREPARE THIS THE NIGHT BEFORE, THEN IT'S JUST A CASE OF DRAGGING YOUR SORRY PARCHED ARSE OVER TO THE FREEZER, NECKING THE GRANITA, AND COOLING YOUR BOOZE-FRIED BRAIN.

6 cups (1½ liters) fruit juice or purée of your choice, such as mango, cranberry, or organic apple juice

sugar, to taste

**serves 4**

★ Add sugar so that the juice is just a little sweeter than you like to drink it (freezing reduces sweetness). Fill ice cube trays with the fruit juice. Freeze.

★ When ready to serve, turn out into 4 small bowls and crush with a fork—you are aiming for an icy texture, not smooth like an ice cream. Serve in small glasses with spoons.

# BLUEBERRY MUESLI SMOOTHIE

WHEN YOU WAKE UP BEFUDDLED FROM BOOZE AND IN NEED OF SERIOUS SUSTENANCE, BUT DON'T HAVE TIME TO MAKE ANYTHING SUBSTANTIAL, THIS SMOOTHIE IS JUST THE THING. SIMPLY BLITZ THE LOT IN A BLENDER AND DRINK THIS MEAL IN A GLASS. FOLLOW IT UP BY NECKING SOME ASPIRIN AND YOU'RE BACK IN BUSINESS.

★ Put all the ingredients in a blender and then blend until smooth.

2 cups (250 g) fresh or frozen blueberries

1 cup (250 ml) yogurt

1 cup (250 ml) milk

⅓ cup (50 g) muesli

1 teaspoon vanilla extract

**serves 2**

# MANGO AND GINGER LASSI

1 cup (250 ml) mango purée, fresh or canned

6 ice cubes

1-in. (2.5-cm) piece fresh ginger, peeled and grated

1 cup (250 ml) low-fat yogurt

mineral water, ginger ale, or milk

sugar or honey, to taste (optional)

4 tablespoons fresh mango, diced, to serve (optional)

**serves 4**

HANGOVER OR NOT, THIS LASSI IS DELICIOUS ANYTIME. THE ALPHONSO MANGO IS RIGHTLY CONSIDERED TO BE THE ABSOLUTE KING OF THE MANGO WORLD, SO, BASED ON THE FACT YOU'RE WORTH IT, USE THE BEST IF YOU CAN FIND THEM. IF NOT, YOU CAN GET TINNED ALPHONSOS IN ASIAN SUPERMARKETS—NOT IDEAL BUT THEY'LL DO. ALTERNATIVELY, USE VERY RIPE REGULAR MANGO AND SPEND AT LEAST AN HOUR CURSING YOUR CRAPPY LUCK AND POOR ACCESS TO PREMIUM PRODUCE.

★ Put all the ingredients except the diced mango in a blender and work to a froth. Serve immediately, topped with the diced mango, if using.

# BANANA BREAKFAST SMOOTHIE

IF YOU'RE HANGING OUT OF YOUR ASS, OWN A BLENDER, AND LIKE BANANAS, THIS SMOOTHIE IS FOR YOU. IT'S PACKED WITH CALCIUM AND FIBER, WHICH, EVEN IF IT DOESN'T PUT A DENT IN YOUR ACHING MORNING-AFTER HEAD, WILL AT LEAST BE GOOD FOR YOUR TEETH AND MAKE YOU MORE REGULAR. YOU CAN'T LOSE!

★ Put all the ingredients in a blender and blend until smooth. Add extra fruit if preferred.

1 cup (250 ml) 1% (low-fat) milk

1 cup (250 ml) low-fat yogurt

2 tablespoons crushed ice

1 tablespoon honey

1 banana, peeled and chopped

1 tablespoon wheatgerm (optional)

**serves 2–4**

#  FROZEN BERRY SMOOTHIE

HANGOVERS ARE A YEAR-ROUND PROBLEM. THANKFULLY FROZEN BERRIES ARE A YEAR-ROUND SOLUTION! LET'S ALL RAISE A MIDDLE FINGER TO SEASONALITY (JUST JOKING!). SERIOUSLY THOUGH, THEY CAN BE BLENDED STRAIGHT FROM THE FREEZER, MAKING THIS SMOOTHIE THICK AND INSTANTLY CHILLED. ANOTHER PLUS IS THAT THIS IS A GREAT ONE FOR CHILDREN—HOW MANY KIDS DO YOU KNOW WHO DON'T LIKE ICE CREAM? GET THEM INVOLVED IN YOUR HANGOVER RECOVERY!

1¼ cups (150 g) frozen mixed berries

2 scoops vanilla ice cream

2 cups (500 ml) milk

**serves 2**

★ Put all the ingredients in a blender and then blend until smooth.

# TROPICAL FRUIT SMOOTHIE

## with pineapple, watermelon, strawberries, and lime

THIS TROPICAL-THEMED SMOOTHIE IS PROBABLY THE PERFECT CURE FOR A BANGING MALIBU-INDUCED HANGOVER. YOU CAN GO FREESTYLE WITH THIS ONE AND STICK IN WHATEVER'S GOOD—STAR FRUIT, LYCHEES, AND ANY OTHER IMPROBABLY WEIRD FRUIT YOU CAN LAY YOUR HANDS ON. TAKE CARE NOT TO MIX RED AND GREEN THOUGH, BLITZED UP TOGETHER, THEY MAKE AN UNAPPETIZING GRAY, WHICH IS AESTHETICALLY BAD FOR HANGOVER CURE PURPOSES.

2 limes

10 ice cubes

6 strawberries, hulled

1 small pineapple, peeled, cored, and chopped

¼ watermelon, peeled and deseeded

choice of other fruit such as:

6 canned lychees, drained and deseeded

2 bananas, peeled and sliced

1 apple, deseeded

a handful of berries, such as raspberries or redcurrants

sugar, to taste (optional)

**serves 4–6**

★ Finely slice one of the limes and reserve. Grate the zest and squeeze the juice of the other.

★ Put the ice cubes in a blender and work to a snow. Add all the prepared fruit, in batches if necessary, and blend until smooth. Add the lime zest and juice and blend again. Add sugar, if preferred, then serve in chilled glasses with the slices of lime.

# CHOCOLATE MALT SHAKE

------------------------------------------------

WITH THIS ONE, LET'S FORGET ABOUT ALL THAT HEALTHY HANGOVER CURE PSEUDO-SCIENCE. INSTEAD, MAKE YOURSELF FEEL ALL BETTER WITH A COMFORTING, CALORIE-LADEN, FILTHY CHOCOLATE MALT SHAKE DECORATED WITH MALTESERS! FOR BEST EFFECT, I SUGGEST DRINKING THIS THROUGH A STRAW, WHILE SLUMPED ON THE SOFA IN YOUR DRESSING GOWN WATCHING TRASHY TELEVISION.

4 tablespoons store-bought chocolate syrup

2 cups (500 ml) milk, chilled

¼ cup (30 g) malted milk powder (such as Horlicks or Carnation brand)

4 scoops chocolate ice cream

10 milk chocolate-coated malted milk balls (such as Maltesers), to decorate

2 soda glasses, chilled

a squeezy bottle or piping bag with a small round nozzle/tip

**serves 2**

★ Put two tablespoons of the chocolate syrup in a squeezy bottle or piping bag and drizzle pretty patterns of syrup up the inside of each glass.

★ Put the milk in a blender with the malted milk powder, 2 scoops of the ice cream, and the remaining chocolate syrup. Whizz until very foamy and thick.

★ Cut the malted milk balls in half using a sharp knife. Pour the milkshake into the prepared glasses, top each with a scoop of chocolate ice cream, and decorate with the malted milk balls. Serve immediately.

# PEANUT BUTTER SHAKE

EVERYBODY KNOWS NUTS ARE PRETTY GOOD FOR YOU. I MEAN, HEALTH FOOD SHOPS ARE FULL OF THEM. THEREFORE IT STANDS TO REASON THAT PEANUT BUTTER IS ALMOST DEFINITELY A FANTASTIC HANGOVER CURE. WHAT THE HELL, EVEN IF MY IMPECCABLE LOGIC IS FLAWED AND IT TURNS OUT NOT TO BE, THIS SHAKE SOUNDS SO GOOD THAT YOU SHOULD BE DRINKING ONE OF THESE NO MATTER WHAT YOU FEEL LIKE. UNLESS YOU DON'T LIKE PEANUTS... OR HAVE A NUT ALLERGY... THEN THIS DEFINITELY ISN'T FOR YOU. NO.

2 tablespoons chocolate syrup

4 tablespoons caramel sauce

2 cups (500 ml) milk, chilled

½ cup (100 g) peanut butter

4 scoops vanilla ice cream

1 tablespoon chopped honey-roasted peanuts, to decorate

2 soda glasses, chilled

a squeezy bottle (optional)

**serves 2**

★ Drizzle alternating lines of chocolate syrup and caramel sauce down the inside of each glass using a squeezy bottle or a spoon (use about 1 tablespoon of each sauce per glass).

★ Add the remaining two tablespoons of caramel sauce to a blender with the milk, peanut butter, and two scoops of ice cream and whizz until very foamy and thick.

★ Pour the milkshake into the prepared glasses, top each with a scoop of ice cream, and sprinkle with the peanuts. Serve immediately.

# COFFEE FRAPPÉ

SO, YOU'RE MANAGING THAT HANGOVER PRETTY WELL. THE NAUSEA HAS PASSED, THE HEADACHE IS BUT A DISTANT, DULL THROB, AND YOU CAN ALMOST FUNCTION LIKE A REAL HUMAN AGAIN. EXCEPT YOU'RE FEELING ALL SORRY FOR YOURSELF AND JUST A BIT LETHARGIC. HERE'S WHERE THE COFFEE FRAPPE COMES IN. THE ICE CREAM ELEMENT WILL PUT A SMILE BACK ON THAT GLUM FACE AND THE ESPRESSO PROVIDES THE CAFFEINE JOLT YOU NEED TO WHACK YOUR BODY BACK INTO OVERDRIVE. OH, AND IT TASTES GREAT, TOO.

2 shots espresso, cooled

1½ cups (350 ml) milk

4 scoops coffee ice cream

15 ice cubes

canned whipped cream

unsweetened cocoa powder, for dusting

2 soda glasses, chilled

2 straws

**serves 2**

★ Put the espresso, milk, and 2 scoops of coffee ice cream in a blender with the ice cubes and blitz until thick and creamy. If your blender is not strong enough to crush ice, place the ice cubes in a plastic bag, seal, and wrap in a clean dish towel. Bash the bag with a wooden rolling pin until the ice is crushed, then add to the blender with the other ingredients and blitz together.

★ Pour the milkshake into the chilled glasses and top each glass with a scoop of coffee ice cream. Squirt a little of the cream on top of the shake and dust with cocoa. Serve immediately with straws.

# CHAPTER 2

# BREAKFAST

## CEREAL

LOOK, WE KNOW THAT ONLY THE MOST SEVERE HANGOVER WOULD RENDER SOMEONE INCAPABLE OF MAKING A BOWL OF CEREAL. HAVING SAID THAT, IT WOULDN'T BE RIGHT NOT TO MENTION THE FOOD THAT'S MOST COMMONLY USED TO FIX A BEER-INDUCED SORE HEAD. HERE ARE A FEW FACTS TO READ WHILE MUNCHING YOUR FROSTED FLAKES.

★ According to studies, the average American will chomp their way through 15 lb. (7 kg) of cereal in one year, that's around 160 bowls.

★ Kellogg's Cornflakes are over 100 years old and were invented by Dr John Kellog in the hope that they would reduce the sexual urges he observed in his patients.

★ According to a study by the Environmental Working Group of America, 55.6% of Kellogg's Honey Smacks is sugar. Healthy stuff.

★ Cheerios are the biggest cereal in the US, shifting nearly one billion dollars worth of boxes in 2014.

★ In 1971, General Mills released a strawberry-flavored cereal called Franken Berry. It proved a hit, but also turned kids' poop a worrying shade of pink.

## COFFEE

COFFEE, THE DAILY SAVIOR OF MILLIONS OF HUNGOVER PEOPLE. HOWEVER YOU MAKE YOUR COFFEE, FOLLOW THESE FOUR PRINCIPLES AND YOU WON'T GO FAR WRONG.

★ Fresh beans ground just before brewing make all the difference. Store them in a dark airtight container, in a cool cupboard rather than in the fridge.

★ How finely you grind them depends on what method you are using to make the coffee:
*espresso (including in stove-top pots)*: finely ground
*cafetière*: coarsely ground
*filter (by hand, machine, drip pots, or vacuum pots)*: medium-finely ground
*jug*: coarsely ground

★ Be precise in your measurements. Getting the proper ratio of coffee to water and allowing them to brew together for the right length of time ensures you extract the most character from the beans without the brew becoming bitter.

★ When making espresso, fill the coffee container to the brim and do not compress the grounds, but level them off gently, otherwise the water will not be able to get through them evenly. Fill with water to the mark or rivet.

★ For filter coffee, use 2 tablespoons coffee per ¾ cup (180 ml) water, and brew for 6–8 minutes to extract the full flavor from the beans.

★ Pour the water onto the grounds when it is just off the boil. This is to coax the soluble flavors from the coffee rather than scalding it and turning it bitter. Do not keep coffee warm on the heat or it will become bitter and stewed. Do not reheat previously brewed coffee for the same reason.

# BUTTERMILK PANCAKES

THERE'S A LOT TO BE SAID FOR UTTERLY DECIMATING YOUR HANGOVER IN A DECADENT AND RATHER GLORIOUS FASHION WITH BUTTERMILK PANCAKES. YES, THEY'RE A LITTLE BIT OF EFFORT AND IN YOUR BEFUDDLED STATE YOU'LL PROBABLY GET THE ENTIRE KITCHEN AND YOURSELF SMOTHERED IN FLOUR, EGGS, AND BATTER MIXTURE, BUT YOU'LL ALSO GET A STACK OF THESE GOLDEN DISCS, TOPPED WITH CRISPY BACON (THE HOLY GRAIL OF HANGOVER RECOVERY FOODSTUFFS) AND DRIZZLED WITH MAPLE SYRUP. C'MON! TOTALLY WORTH IT.

★ Sift the flour, baking powder, salt, and sugar into a large mixing bowl and make a well in the middle.

★ Put the milk, buttermilk, eggs, melted butter, and vanilla in small bowl and whisk. Pour into the dry ingredients and whisk until the batter is smooth.

★ Put a tablespoon of butter in a large, heavy skillet (frying pan) and melt over a medium heat, swirling it so that it coats the bottom of the skillet evenly.

★ Drop a ladleful (4 tablespoons) of the pancake batter into the hot skillet and cook for about 1 minute, or until bubbles start to appear on the surface. Using a spatula or palette knife, flip the pancake over and cook the other side until the pancake is golden and well risen. Remove the pancake from the skillet and keep it warm on a plate covered with foil.

★ Repeat with the remaining batter.

★ Serve the pancakes with crisp bacon, if you like, and a drizzle of maple syrup.

1¾ cups (225 g) all-purpose (plain) flour

3 teaspoons baking powder

½ teaspoon salt

¼ cup (50 g) superfine (caster) sugar

½ cup (125 ml) milk

½ cup (125 ml) buttermilk

2 eggs, lightly beaten

3 tablespoons (45 g) unsalted butter, melted, plus extra for frying

1 teaspoon vanilla extract

pure maple syrup, to serve

crispy cooked bacon slices, to serve (optional)

**makes 16–18**

# BLUEBERRY PANCAKES

## with maple syrup pecans

THERE YOU WERE TRYING TO LIVE A HEALTHY LIFESTYLE THIS MONTH, BUT THE TEMPTATION OF AFTER-WORK FRIDAY DRINKS GOT THE BETTER OF YOU. FEAR NOT, BECAUSE THESE PANCAKES HAVE BLUEBERRIES, CONSIDERED BY MANY LEADING EXPERTS TO BE THE ULTIMATE SUPERFOOD, SO DON'T FEEL GUILTY ABOUT THOSE BEERS LAST NIGHT. SEE, EVERYTHING BALANCES ITSELF OUT IN THE END, YOU CLEAN-LIVING, VIRTUOUS THING, YOU.

★ Preheat the oven to 400°F (200°C) Gas 6.

★ To make the maple syrup pecans, spread the pecan halves over a baking sheet and cook in the preheated oven for 5 minutes until lightly toasted. Simmer the maple syrup in a small saucepan for 3 minutes. Remove from the heat and stir in the pecans and butter.

★ To make the pancakes, sift the flour, baking powder, salt, and sugar into a bowl. Put the egg yolks, sour cream, milk, and butter into a second bowl and beat well, then add the flour mixture all at once and beat until smooth. Put the egg whites into a clean bowl and beat until soft peaks form. Fold them gently into the batter, then fold in the blueberries. (Don't overmix—some lumps of flour and egg white don't matter.)

★ Lightly grease a skillet (frying pan) and preheat over medium heat. Reduce the heat. Pour 3 tablespoons of batter into the pan and cook in batches of 3–4 for 1–2 minutes over very low heat to avoid burning the blueberries, until small bubbles begin to appear on top and the underside is golden brown. Turn them over and cook the other side for 1 minute. Transfer to a plate and keep them warm in a low oven while you cook the remainder.

★ Serve with ice cream and the maple syrup pecans.

---

1½ cups (285 g) all-purpose (plain) flour

2 teaspoons baking powder

1 teaspoon salt

¼ cup (55 g) superfine (caster) sugar

2 eggs, separated

1 cup (250 ml) sour cream

⅔ cup (150 ml) milk

4 tablespoons (55 g) unsalted butter, melted and cooled

2 cups (250 g) blueberries, fresh or frozen

vanilla ice cream, to serve

**maple syrup pecans**

¾ cup (100 g) pecan halves

1 cup (250 ml) maple syrup

4 tablespoons (55 g) unsalted butter

**makes 8–10 pancakes**

# TRIPLE CHOCOLATE PANCAKES

SOMETIMES YOU JUST TO NEED TO CURE YOURSELF WITH INDULGENCE AND THESE PANCAKES CERTAINLY DO THE JOB. NOT ONE, NOT TWO, BUT *THREE* TYPES OF CHOCOLATE ARE REPRESENTED HERE. YES, THERE ARE PROBABLY MORE CALORIES IN THIS THAN ANY HUMAN CAN SAFELY INGEST, BUT TRIPLE CHOCOLATE—I THINK THAT SAYS IT ALL.

1½ cups (285 g) all-purpose (plain) flour

¼ cup (75 g) cocoa powder

1 teaspoon baking powder

1 teaspoon baking (bicarbonate of) soda

¼ cup (55 g) superfine (caster) sugar

¾ cup (200 ml) milk

½ cup (125 ml) buttermilk

2 eggs, separated

2 tablespoons (30 g) unsalted butter, melted and cooled

½ teaspoon salt

3 oz. (100 g) bittersweet (dark) chocolate, chopped

3 oz. (100 g) white chocolate, chopped

chocolate sauce, to serve (optional)

**white chocolate yogurt**

6 oz. (150 g) white chocolate

4 tablespoons Greek yogurt

**makes about 12 pancakes**

★ Sift the flour, cocoa, baking powder, baking (bicarbonate of) soda, and sugar into a bowl. Put the milk, buttermilk, egg yolks, and butter into a second large bowl and beat well. Add the flour mixture and mix thoroughly.

★ Put the egg whites and salt into a clean bowl and beat until stiff peaks form. Add 1 tablespoon of the egg whites to the pancake mixture and stir to loosen it, then carefully fold in the remaining egg whites, then the bittersweet (dark) and white chocolate.

★ Lightly grease a stove-top grill-pan or skillet (frying pan) and warm over medium heat. Reduce the heat. Pour about 2 tablespoons of batter into the pan and cook in batches of 3–4 over low heat for about 1 minute, or until small bubbles begin to appear on the surface and the underside is golden brown. Turn the pancakes over and cook the other side for 1 minute. Transfer to a plate and keep them warm in a low oven while you cook the remainder.

★ To make the white chocolate yogurt, put the chocolate into a bowl set over a saucepan of simmering water and melt slowly. Remove from the heat and leave to cool a little, then beat in the yogurt until the mixture is smooth and shiny. Serve with the pancakes and chocolate sauce, if using.

# MORNING-AFTER BREAKFAST WAFFLES

I DON'T KNOW ABOUT YOU, BUT I RECKON THE IDEA OF A CRISP WAFFLE THAT'S OOZING CHEESE AND IS PILED WITH ROASTED TOMATOES, EGGS, AND BACON SOUNDS LIKE THE BEST THING EVER! OK, YOU'RE GOING TO NEED A WAFFLE IRON TO PRODUCE THE GOODS, BUT SERIOUSLY, THIS RECIPE ALONE IS WORTH THE OUTLAY. IF YOU'RE REALLY HUNGRY, FEEL FREE TO SLING SOME OTHER BREAKFAST STAPLES ONTO THE TOP. I THINK A FEW SAUSAGES AND SOME FRIED MUSHROOMS WOULDN'T BE UNWELCOME ADDITIONS.

¾ cup plus 2 tablespoons (180 g) all-purpose (plain) flour

¾ cup (120 g) fine cornmeal

2 teaspoons baking powder

½ teaspoon sea salt

2 eggs, separated

1 cup (225 ml) milk

¾ cup (200 ml) sour cream or yogurt

2 tablespoons olive oil, plus extra for frying and roasting

1⅓ cups (120 g) grated Cheddar cheese

2 tablespoons snipped fresh chives

**to serve**

20 cherry tomatoes, on the vine

16 bacon slices

8 eggs

sea salt and freshly ground pepper

**makes 8 waffles**

★ Preheat the oven to 400°F (200°C) Gas 6 and grease a baking sheet. Lightly grease and preheat the waffle iron.

★ Put the vine tomatoes on the prepared baking sheet, sprinkle with olive oil, season, and roast for 5 minutes or until their skins blister.

★ To make the waffles, sift the flour, cornmeal, baking powder, and salt in a large bowl. Put the egg yolks into another bowl, add the milk, sour cream, and olive oil and beat well. Add the flour mixture and beat well. Put the egg whites in a clean bowl and beat until stiff peaks form. Using a large metal spoon, gently fold the egg whites, Cheddar, and chives into the batter.

★ Brush a small skillet (frying pan) with olive oil and heat well. Add the bacon and fry until crisp. Remove from the skillet and leave to drain on paper towels. Brush the skillet with oil again, add 4 slices of the cooked bacon, then break 2 eggs on top and fry gently until the eggs are done. Set aside to keep warm.

★ Spoon ½ cup (125 ml) of batter into the preheated waffle iron compartments. Adjust the amount of batter according to the size of your iron. Cook until crisp, at least 4–5 minutes (cheese waffles taste so much better when well done). Transfer to a plate, slide the bacon and eggs on top, and serve with the tomatoes. Repeat to make the other servings.

# BELGIAN WAFFLES
with strawberries and praline cream

I THINK IT'S FAIR TO SAY THE BELGIANS KNOW A THING OR TWO ABOUT BREWING BEER... AND DEALING WITH THE SUBSEQUENT AFTER EFFECTS THE NEXT DAY. THEIR CONTRIBUTION, THE CLASSIC BELGIAN WAFFLE, THICK WITH DEEP WELLS TO TRAP BUTTER AND SYRUP, IS A PERFECT EXAMPLE OF WHAT TO EAT WHEN YOU'RE FEELING FRAGILE. HOLY MOLY! YES!

2 cups (285 g) all-purpose (plain) flour

2 tablespoons superfine (caster) sugar

1 teaspoon salt

1 teaspoon active (easy-blend) dry yeast

1½ sticks (140 g) unsalted butter, melted and cooled

1½ cups (375 ml) milk

1 teaspoon vanilla extract

3 eggs, separated

8 oz. (250 g) strawberries, to serve

maple syrup and/or butter, to serve (optional)

**praline cream**

1¼ cups (300 ml) heavy (double) cream

2 oz. (55 g) store-bought hazelnut brittle, ground to a powder

**makes 12 waffles**

★ Start the day before. Sift the flour, sugar, salt, and yeast into a large bowl. Stir in the butter, milk, and vanilla extract to make a smooth mixture. Cover the bowl with plastic wrap and leave at room temperature overnight.

★ In the morning, lightly grease the waffle iron and preheat. Beat the egg yolks into the yeast mixture. Put the egg whites into a clean, grease-free bowl and beat with a wire whisk until stiff peaks form. Carefully fold them into the batter with a metal spoon.

★ To make the praline cream, put the cream into a clean bowl and whip to a soft, loose consistency. Stir in the ground hazelnut brittle.

★ Pour about ½ cup (125 ml) batter into the preheated waffle iron compartments. Adjust the amount of batter according to the size of your iron. Cook until golden, 3–5 minutes. The waffles should be crisp on the outside and served immediately. They can be kept warm in a low oven, but will lose some crispness. A quick reheating in the toaster works remarkably well.

★ Serve the waffles hot with a spoonful of the praline cream and a few fresh strawberries. Or if you think that's unnecessary effort and fanciness, drizzle with maple syrup or butter (or both).

# HASH BROWNS
## with sausages and roasted tomatoes

I LOVE POTATOES AT ANY TIME, BUT IN THEIR FRIED, GOLDEN "HASH BROWN" GUISE, THEY ARE ABSOLUTELY SUPERB AT HELPING YOU GET OVER THAT UTTERLY WASHED OUT, "WHY THE HELL DID I DRINK SAMBUCA LAST NIGHT?" FEELING. HERE, THE ADDITION OF ROASTED TOMATOES AND SAUSAGES MAKE THE CURE COMPLETE. ALTERNATIVELY, SOME CRISPY BACON AND A POACHED EGG OR TWO SLUNG ON TOP OF YOUR HASH BROWNS MAKE A CRACKING PLAN B.

★ Preheat the oven to 400°F (200°C) Gas 6. Lightly grease a baking sheet.

★ Cook the potatoes in a large saucepan of lightly salted boiling water for 10–12 minutes, until almost cooked through. Drain and mash roughly.

★ Melt the butter in a large, non-stick skillet (frying pan) and gently fry the onion for 15 minutes, until soft and golden. Add the potatoes and seasoning. Cook, stirring and mashing the potatoes occasionally, for about 15–20 minutes, or until well browned and crispy around the edges.

★ Meanwhile, put the sausages in a roasting pan, drizzle with half the oil, and roast on the middle shelf of the preheated oven for 25 minutes.

★ Once the sausages are in the oven, put the tomatoes on the prepared baking sheet. Drizzle with the remaining oil and put on the top shelf of the oven after the sausages have been cooking for 5 minutes. Cook for about 15 minutes, then drizzle over the balsamic vinegar and cook for a further 5 minutes.

★ Spoon the hash browns onto plates and top with the sausages and tomatoes.

1½ lb. (750 g) floury potatoes, diced

4 tablespoons (50 g) butter

1 large onion, finely chopped

12 premium sausages

2 tablespoons olive oil

20 cherry tomatoes, on the vine

1 tablespoon balsamic vinegar

sea salt and freshly ground black pepper

**serves 4**

# FRENCH TOAST

PREPARE TO HAVE YOUR MIND BLOWN. ARE YOU SITTING DOWN? OK. FRENCH TOAST... ISN'T ACTUALLY FROM FRANCE! WHAT THE HELL, RIGHT? APPARENTLY, IT'S ORIGINALLY ROMAN IN ORIGIN. *C'EST INCREDIBLE!* ANYWAY, WHEREVER IT'S FROM, IT'S A GREAT, EASY, AND SWEET WAY TO SOAK UP THE BOOZE FROM THE NIGHT BEFORE. IF YOU'RE FEELING PARTICULARLY FLUSH OR IN NEED OF DECADENCE, USE BRIOCHE AND DAMN THE CALORIES!

4 thick slices white bread or brioche

2 large eggs, beaten

2 tablespoons light (single) cream

½ teaspoon vanilla extract

3½ tablespoons raw (golden caster) sugar

3 tablespoons (45 g) unsalted butter, for frying

½ teaspoon ground cinnamon

maple syrup, to serve (optional)

**serves 4**

★ Trim the crusts from the bread, then cut the slices in half. Put the eggs, cream, vanilla extract, and 1 teaspoon of the sugar in a shallow dish and mix with a fork.

★ Heat half the butter in a large, heavy, non-stick skillet (frying pan). When the butter is foaming, thoroughly coat a piece of bread in the egg mixture, drain off the excess, and put it in the hot butter. Add 3 more pieces of coated bread to the skillet in the same way, then cook over medium heat for 3–4 minutes until the underside is golden brown. Turn over and cook the other side. Meanwhile, mix the remaining sugar and cinnamon in a small sugar shaker or bowl. Put the cooked bread on a warm serving plate and sprinkle with some of the cinnamon sugar.

★ Wipe out the skillet, reheat, and cook the remaining pieces of bread as before. Serve hot, sprinkled with more cinnamon sugar and maple syrup, if using.

## Variation

To make cinnamon toast, heat the broiler (grill), toast thick slices of bread on both sides, then butter thoroughly. Mix the cinnamon sugar as in the recipe above, and sprinkle generously to cover. Put the toast back under the broiler until the sugar starts to melt and bubble. Remove carefully and eat when the toast has cooled enough not to burn your lips.

# BREAKFAST KEBABS

IF YOU'RE ANYTHING LIKE ME, THE CRUEL IRONY OF THIS RECIPE IS YOU'VE PROBABLY SPENT HALF THE MORNING VIOLENTLY BARKING UP LAST NIGHT'S KEBAB, ONLY TO BE MAKING THIS RECIPE AND EATING ANOTHER FOR BREAKFAST. ALTHOUGH TO BE FAIR, THIS ONE, WHICH IS PACKED WITH CHARGRILLED VEGETABLES, WILL BE MUCH, MUCH NICER AND HEALTHIER THAN THE ELEPHANT LEG YOU WERE DRUNKENLY MUNCHING ON WHILE INEBRIATED. PROMISE.

★ Preheat the oven to 425°F (220°C) Gas 7 and grease a large roasting pan.

★ Deseed the peppers then cut them into large chunks. Cut each slice of bacon in half, then roll up. Cut the onion into quarters. Leave the tomatoes and sausages whole.

★ Thread the peppers, bacon, onion, tomatoes, and sausages onto the wooden skewers, leaving a small gap between each piece on the skewer. Put them in any order you like, but make sure each skewer has an equal amount of each ingredient.

★ Arrange the kebabs in the prepared roasting pan, slightly apart. Bake for 15–20 minutes, or until golden. Meanwhile, warm the bread rolls, either in the toaster or in a second oven on a low temperature. Put a kebab on each serving plate and serve immediately with the warmed bread.

½ red bell pepper

½ green bell pepper

½ yellow bell pepper

4 back bacon slices

1 small red onion

8 cherry tomatoes or baby plum tomatoes

8 small cocktail sausages

4 soft whole-wheat (wholemeal) rolls or pita breads

4 wooden skewers, soaked in warm water for 10 minutes

**makes 4 kebabs**

# RAREBIT

WITH REGARD TO HANGOVERS, I'M A FIRM
BELIEVER THAT THE UNHEALTHIER THE
BREAKFAST, THE GREATER THE RESTORATIVE
EFFECT. WITH THIS IN MIND, CHEESE ON
TOAST IS A WINNER. AT THIS POINT
YOU'RE PROBABLY SCRATCHING YOUR
HEAD, THINKING, "CHEESE ON TOAST?!
I DON'T NEED A RECIPE FOR THAT, EVEN IF
I AM ABSOLUTELY HANGING," AND YOU'D
BE RIGHT. BUT THIS IS RAREBIT, AKA POSH
CHEESE ON TOAST—IT'S LOVELY AND HAS
BEEN KNOCKING AROUND SINCE THE
SIXTEENTH CENTURY, SO GO MAKE SOME.

1½ tablespoons (25 g) butter

4 shallots or 1 onion, sliced

1 cup (100 g) grated Cheddar or Gruyère cheese

⅓ cup (75 ml) ale or lager

1 teaspoon mustard

a pinch of sea salt

2 eggs, lightly beaten

4 slices bread

freshly ground black pepper

**serves 2–4**

★ Melt the butter in a heavy-based saucepan, add the shallots, and cook until softened. Add the cheese, ale, mustard, and salt. Stir over low heat until the cheese has melted.

★ Add the beaten eggs and stir until the mixture has thickened slightly, about 2–3 minutes. Don't overcook it or you will end up with scrambled eggs.

★ Meanwhile, toast the bread on both sides, then spoon the cheese mixture onto the toast and cook under a hot broiler (grill) until puffed and gold-flecked. Serve with lots of black pepper.

# THE HOT BROWN

IF I TOLD YOU THAT AFTER A HEAVY NIGHT WHAT YOU SHOULD BE WAKING UP TO IS A "HOT BROWN," YOU MAY BE A LITTLE DISTRESSED. FEAR NOT, I'M NOT ADVOCATING A DRINK-INDUCED STUPOR LEADING TO AN INVOLUNTARILY INCIDENT IN YOUR PJ'S. NO, A HOT BROWN IS A SANDWICH CONSISTING OF BUTTERED AND GRILLED "TEXAS TOAST" (BREAD CUT TO DOUBLE THICKNESS) TOPPED WITH TURKEY AND BACON, AND SMOTHERED IN A CHEESY MORNAY SAUCE. SHOULD YOU REALLY THINK ABOUT EATING ANYTHING ELSE?

## mornay sauce

3 tablespoons (45 g) butter

⅓ cup (40 g) all-purpose (plain) flour

scant 2 cups (450 ml) warmed milk

1 cup (115 g) grated Gruyère cheese, plus extra to garnish

sea salt and black pepper, to taste

## Texas toast

loaf of white bread

butter, at room temperature

6 slices cold cooked turkey breast

4 slices broiled (grilled) bacon, kept hot

a pinch of paprika, to garnish

fresh flat-leaf parsley, finely chopped, to garnish

**serves 2**

★ To make the mornay sauce, melt the butter in a saucepan, then mix in the flour, stirring well to form a thick paste (or roux). Cook this over a fairly gentle heat for a couple of minutes, stirring constantly and taking care not to color the roux. Gradually whisk in the warmed milk and cook the sauce over a medium heat until it comes to a boil—about 3 minutes. Reduce the heat to a simmer and season with salt and pepper. Whisk in the grated cheese until melted. Remove from the heat.

★ Preheat the broiler (grill) to high.

★ Make the "Texas toast" by cutting 4 slices from a loaf of white bread to twice the thickness of regular slices, then buttering both sides and broiling (grilling) each slice until crisp and golden on both sides.

★ To assemble the hot browns, place a slice of "Texas toast" in each of 2 heatproof dishes. Top each with 3 slices of turkey breast and pour some mornay sauce over each. Sprinkle with extra cheese to garnish.

★ Put under the hot broiler until the cheese is melted and everything is bubbling.

★ Remove from the broiler and top each with 2 slices of hot crispy bacon, then sprinkle with paprika and parsley. Serve the remaining 2 slices of toast on the side.

# EGGS BENEDICT

AN ABSOLUTELY CLASSIC FOR YOUR SOPHISTICATED HANGOVER, NO DOUBT INFLICTED BY CHAMPAGNE OR, IF YOU'RE LESS CLASSY, CHEAP LAMBRUSCO. I WON'T JUDGE YOUR CHOICES (MUCH!); WHAT I WILL TELL YOU IS THAT HOLLANDAISE SAUCE IS GORGEOUS, BUT HAS A TENDENCY TO SPLIT LIKE A BASTARD. IF IT DOES (AND CONSIDERING THAT YOU'RE FEELING ROUGH WHILST COOKING THIS, IT DEFINITELY WILL), TAKE THE SAUCE OFF THE HEAT AND WHISK IN A TABLESPOON OF COLD WATER. REPEAT UNTIL IT COMES TOGETHER AGAIN. FIXED!

**hollandaise sauce**

2 sticks (250 g) unsalted butter

3 egg yolks

1 teaspoon freshly squeezed lemon juice

sea salt and freshly ground black pepper

4 large slices prosciutto

4 eggs

1 tablespoon vinegar (preferably distilled)

4 English muffins

**serves 4**

★ To make the hollandaise sauce, put the butter in a small saucepan and melt it gently over very low heat, without letting it brown. Put the egg yolks, 2 tablespoons water, and lemon juice in a blender and process until frothy. With the blade turning, gradually pour in the melted butter in a steady stream until the sauce is thickened and glossy. Transfer the sauce to a bowl set over a saucepan of hot water. Cover and keep the sauce warm.

★ Broil (grill) or sauté the slices of prosciutto until really crisp and keep them warm in a low oven. To poach the eggs, bring a saucepan of lightly salted water to the boil. Add the vinegar and reduce to a gentle simmer. Swirl the water well with a fork and crack 2 eggs into the water. Cook for 3 minutes, remove with a slotted spoon, and repeat with the remaining 2 eggs.

★ Meanwhile, toast the muffins whole and top each with a slice of crisp prosciutto. Put the poached eggs on top of the ham. Spoon over the hollandaise, sprinkle with seasoning, and serve at once.

# EGGS FLORENTINE

IF YOU'RE SUFFERING AFTER A NIGHT ON THE SAUCE AND YOU'RE A VEGETARIAN, THEN SADLY EGGS BENEDICT ARE NOT FOR YOU. HOWEVER, DON'T BE SAD; CHUCK OUT THE HAM, THROW SOME SPINACH ON TOP INSTEAD, AND YOU'VE GOT EGGS FLORENTINE! THE VEGETABLE ELEMENT HERE IS PRESUMABLY ALSO INCREDIBLY GOOD FOR YOUR ACHING INTERNAL BITS, TOO. LET'S JUST IGNORE ALL THAT BUTTER IN THE HOLLANDAISE, EH?

★ To poach the eggs, bring a saucepan of lightly salted water to the boil. Add the vinegar and reduce to a gentle simmer. Swirl the water well with a fork and crack the eggs into the water. Cook for 3 minutes and remove with a slotted spoon.

★ Meanwhile, melt the butter in a saucepan, then add the spinach. Cook for about 3 minutes, stirring occasionally, until the spinach begins to wilt. Season with nutmeg and salt and pepper. Remove from the heat, cover, and keep it warm.

★ Toast the muffins whole and spread with butter. Spoon some spinach onto each muffin (taking care to drain off any excess liquid as you do so). Set an egg on top, spoon over the hollandaise sauce, sprinkle with a little more pepper, and serve immediately.

2 eggs

1 tablespoon vinegar (preferably distilled)

1 tablespoon (15 g) butter, plus extra to spread

8 oz. (200 g) baby spinach leaves

a pinch of freshly grated nutmeg

2 English muffins

2–4 tablespoons hollandaise sauce (page 30)

sea salt and freshly ground black pepper

**serves 2**

# HUEVOS RANCHEROS

SOME OF MY WORST EVER HANGOVERS HAVE INVOLVED THAT MOST MEXICAN OF AWFUL SPIRITS, CHEAP TEQUILA. SO IT STANDS TO REASON THAT HUEVOS RANCHEROS, THAT MOST MEXICAN OF AWFULLY AMAZING BREAKFASTS (SEE WHAT I DID THERE?) IS THE PERFECT ANTIDOTE TO A NIGHT NECKING THAT HELLISH BOOZE. TO INCREASE THE CHANCE THAT YOU'LL ACTUALLY KNOCK THIS DISH UP FOR BREAKFAST, MAKE THE SALSA THE DAY BEFORE.

4 corn tortillas

3 tablespoons vegetable oil

1 cup (90 g) grated mild cheese, such as Cheddar or Monterey Jack

4 eggs

sea salt and freshly ground pepper

**salsa**

6 plum tomatoes, halved

2 jalapeño peppers

8 garlic cloves, unpeeled

¼ cup (4 tablespoons) chopped cilantro (coriander)

1 teaspoon Tabasco Sauce or favorite hot sauce

1 small red onion, finely chopped, to serve

**serves 4**

★ To make the salsa, place the halved tomatoes cut-side up in a shallow roasting pan. Season and place on the top rack under a preheated broiler (grill). Broil (grill) for about 10 minutes, or until charred.

★ Preheat the oven to 400°F (200°C) Gas 6.

★ Meanwhile, in a dry, non-stick skillet (frying pan), blacken the peppers and garlic cloves. Keep turning to color all sides. When done, peel the garlic and place in a food processor. Put the peppers in a plastic bag, tie a knot in the bag, and leave the peppers to steam for a few minutes, then peel, deseed, and stem. Add the flesh to the food processor along with the tomatoes, 2 tablespoons of cilantro (coriander), and the Tabasco. Season and pulse until smooth. Pour into a pan and cook briefly over medium heat to warm through.

★ Brush the tortillas with 2 tablespoons of the oil and bake for 5 minutes until golden. Divide the cheese between the tortillas and return to the oven for 5 minutes until the cheese has melted. Turn off the oven, open the door and leave the tortillas in to keep warm. Fry the eggs in a non-stick skillet in the remaining tablespoon of oil. Place the tortillas on 4 plates and slip an egg on top of each. Spoon the warm salsa over each and sprinkle with the chopped onion and remaining cilantro.

# ULTIMATE OMELET

## with sausage, potato, and onion

A REGULAR OMELET IS FAR TOO INSUBSTANTIAL TO MAKE EVEN A TINY
DENT IN ANYTHING BUT THE MILDEST HANGOVER. THIS ULTIMATE
OMELET HOWEVER IS RIPPED SILLY; STUFFED TO PERFECTION WITH
EVERYTHING YOU NEED TO FIGHT THE EFFECTS OF ALCOHOL EXCESS.
IF THAT'S STILL NOT ENOUGH, GO CRAZY AND MAKE THE "ULTIMATE-
ULTIMATE" OMELET—ADD A HANDFUL OF GRATED CHEDDAR, CHOPPED
TOMATOES, CHILI, AND ANY COOKED SAUSAGE (FRANKFURTER,
CHORIZO ETC) YOU CAN LAY YOUR HANDS ON. IT'S THE WAY TO GO.

★ Heat 1 tablespoon of the oil in a heavy, non-stick skillet (frying pan).
Add the sausages and fry for 8–10 minutes, turning them frequently.
Remove and set aside. Wipe out the skillet with paper towels.

★ Heat 2 tablespoons of oil in the cleaned skillet. Add the
potatoes, layering them with the onions. Cook for 10–15 minutes
over medium-low heat, lifting and turning occasionally, until just
tender. The potatoes and onions should not brown much.

★ Break the eggs into a large bowl, add salt and pepper, and
beat briefly with a fork. Remove the potatoes and onions from
the skillet and add to the egg mixture. Thickly slice the
sausages and mix with the eggs and potatoes.

★ Return the skillet to the heat, adding a little more oil if
necessary. Add the potato and egg mixture spreading it evenly.
Cook over medium-low heat until the bottom is golden brown
and the top has almost set.

★ Put a plate on top of the skillet, then invert so the omelet
drops onto the plate. Slide back into the skillet, brown-side up,
and cook for 2–3 minutes until lightly browned underneath.
Serve hot or warm, cut into wedges.

3–4 tablespoons extra virgin olive or
sunflower oil

6 pork chipolata sausages with herbs

1 onion, halved and cut into slivers

3 potatoes, about 12 oz. (325 g), thinly
sliced

5 extra-large eggs (large if in the UK)

sea salt and freshly ground black
pepper

serves 2–3

# EGGS COCOTTE

EGGS COCOTTE, OR BAKED EGGS, IS A BIT SOPHISTICATED, WHICH, IF YOU'RE
READING THIS BOOK, IS SOMETHING I SUSPECT YOU'RE NOT. I'M JOKING
OF COURSE (I'M NOT!), BUT IGNORING CASUAL INSULTS, THIS DISH HAS
ATTRIBUTES THAT ANYONE WHO'S EVER WOKEN UP UTTERLY BROKEN AND IN
NEED OF BREAKFAST CAN APPRECIATE. IT'S QUICK, CHEAP, AND STUPIDLY
EASY. JUST LIKE YOU! I'M NOT EVEN GOING TO PRETEND I'M JOKING THIS TIME.

★ Preheat the oven to 400°F (200°C) Gas 6.

★ Divide the spinach between 4 greased ovenproof ramekins. Crack an egg on
top, add a spoonful of milk to each, then season and top with the Parmesan. Put
the ramekins on a baking sheet in the preheated oven and cook for 6 minutes.

2 oz. (60 g) fresh
spinach, chopped

4 eggs

4 tablespoons milk

¾ cup (75 g) grated
Parmesan cheese

sea salt and freshly ground
black pepper

**serves 4**

# THE FULL ENGLISH

NOW WE'RE TALKING. THIS IS THE UNDISPUTED KING OF HANGOVER BREAKFASTS. WHEN YOU'VE CRAWLED OUT OF WHATEVER GUTTER YOU'VE SPENT THE NIGHT IN, REEKING OF BOOZE AND FEELING LIKE YOU WISH YOU WERE DEAD, THIS WILL SEE YOU RIGHT. MAKE SURE YOU USE GOOD-QUALITY SAUSAGES AND BACON—NO PIG LIPS OR EYELIDS THANKS VERY MUCH. ENGLISH MUSTARD ON THE SIDE IS A MUST, AS IS A MUG OF TEA. ABSOLUTELY SUPERB.

★ Preparation is both easy and greasy. Grab a large skillet (frying pan), add the oil, and fry all the ingredients—except the baked beans—over medium heat.

★ Timing is key, so start with the sausages, which take the longest to cook (around 15 minutes), turning regularly. Next come the bacon, tomatoes, and mushrooms, then finish by frying the eggs.

★ Once the bacon has been added, heat up the baked beans in a separate saucepan.

★ Transfer everything to plates and serve with buttered bread and cups of tea.

★ If you're feeling adventurous, you can even include black pudding. (That's congealed pig's blood served in a pig's intestine, in case you're asking.)

1 tablespoon vegetable oil

4 sausages

4 bacon slices

2 tomatoes, halved

a handful button mushrooms, halved

2 eggs

1 14-oz. (400-g) can baked beans

2 slices bread, buttered

2 cups of tea with milk and sugar

2 slices black pudding (optional)

**serves 2**

# CORNED BEEF HASH

THIS TWIST ON THAT CLASSIC BRITISH LEFTOVER DISH, BUBBLE AND SQUEAK, IS PERFECT HANGOVER FODDER. OTHER BONUSES ARE IT'S DIRT CHEAP AND IT'S MORE OR LESS ONE-PAN COOKING, SO NOT MUCH WASHING UP. ALSO, IF YOU'VE GOT LEFTOVER SPUDS IN THE FRIDGE, SLING THEM IN INSTEAD OF COOKING SOME SPECIALLY... EVEN EASIER.

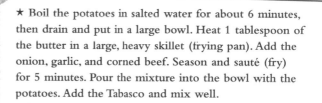

3 baking potatoes (around 1½ lb./700 g), peeled and diced

3 tablespoons (45 g) butter

1 onion, diced

1 garlic clove, finely chopped

10 oz. (300 g) cooked corned beef brisket, diced

½ teaspoon Tabasco sauce

1 tablespoon vegetable oil

4 eggs

**serves 4**

★ Boil the potatoes in salted water for about 6 minutes, then drain and put in a large bowl. Heat 1 tablespoon of the butter in a large, heavy skillet (frying pan). Add the onion, garlic, and corned beef. Season and sauté (fry) for 5 minutes. Pour the mixture into the bowl with the potatoes. Add the Tabasco and mix well.

★ Add the remaining butter to the skillet. Pour the potato mixture into it and press everything down firmly. Cover with a heavy lid or plate that will fit just inside the pan to weight the mixture down. Cook over a medium heat for 10 minutes. Turn the mixture over in batches and cook for 10 minutes on the other side. The meat should be brown and crisp; keep cooking and turning if it isn't.

★ Make 4 indentations in the potatoes and crack an egg into each. Place a fitted lid over the pan and cook until the eggs are done. Alternatively, in a separate non-stick skillet, heat 1 tablespoon vegetable oil and fry the eggs. Place one fried egg on top of each serving of corned beef hash. You can also poach the eggs instead of frying them.

# BRUNCH QUESADILLAS

WE'RE MEXICO-BOUND FOR THIS HANGOVER CURE... SORT OF. BAKED BEANS PROBABLY AREN'T THE MOST AUTHENTIC INGREDIENT, BUT A LOT OF US WILL HAVE A CAN SAT IN A CUPBOARD. IF YOU'VE GOT SOME REFRIED BEANS, USE THOSE FOR AUTHENTICITY (YOU PROBABLY WON'T HAVE). ANYWAY, IT'S BASICALLY A FRIED HAM, CHEESE, AND BEAN SANDWICH TOPPED WITH AN EGG. I CAN'T KNOCK THAT, SO I WON'T.

★ Preheat the oven to 250°F (120°C) Gas ½.

★ To assemble the quesadillas, put 1 slice of ham on each of the 4 tortillas. Sprinkle each with a quarter of the cheese and spoon over a quarter of the baked beans, then top with another tortilla.

★ Heat the oil in a non-stick skillet (frying pan) over medium heat. When hot, add a quesadilla, lower the heat, and cook for 2–3 minutes until golden on one side and the cheese begins to melt. Turn over and cook the other side for 2–3 minutes. Transfer to a heatproof plate and keep warm in the preheated oven while you cook the rest.

★ Melt 1 tablespoon of the butter in a small non-stick skillet (frying pan). Add 1 egg and fry until cooked through, turning once to cook both sides if desired. Repeat to cook the remaining eggs.

★ To serve, top each quesadilla with a fried egg. Cut into wedges and serve immediately.

4 thick slices ham

8 large flour tortillas

2 cups (200 g) grated Cheddar or Monterey Jack cheese

1 14-oz. (400-g) can baked beans

1 tablespoon vegetable oil

3 tablespoons (45 g) butter

4 eggs

**serves 4–6**

# CHAPTER 3

# QUICK FIXES

# BASIC GRILLED CHEESE SANDWICH

HAVE YOU SEEN THAT SCENE IN THE FILM *CHEF* WHERE JON FAVREAU MAKES A GRILLED CHEESE SANDWICH? IT'S INSANE. I DEFY ANYONE TO WATCH IT AND NOT BE GAGGING FOR ONE. IT'S FOOD PORN OF THE HIGHEST ORDER AND PRETTY MUCH WHAT YOU'RE GOING TO RECREATE HERE. CRISP FRIED BREAD AND OOZING MELTED CHEESE... HELL YES! IF THIS DOESN'T SORT YOUR HANGOVER OUT, I DON'T KNOW WHAT WILL. BY THE WAY, THERE IS MUCH ROOM FOR EXPERIMENTING HERE—I RECKON SLICED LEEKS, ONIONS, TOMATOES, AND HOT SAUCE COULD ONLY MAKE THIS BETTER. GO NUTS.

4 large slices white bread

unsalted butter, softened

3¼ cups (300 g) mixed mild cheeses, such as Cheddar, Gruyère, Monterey Jack, or Gouda, grated

**serves 2**

★ Butter each of the bread slices on one side and arrange them buttered-side down on a clean work surface or chopping board.

★ It's best to assemble the sandwiches in a large, non-stick skillet (frying pan) before you heat it up. Start by putting two slices of bread in the skillet, butter-side down. If you can only accommodate one slice in your pan, you'll need to cook one sandwich at a time. Top each slice with half of the grated cheese, but be careful not to let too much cheese fall into the pan. Top with the final pieces of bread, butter-side up.

★ Turn the heat to medium and cook for 3–4 minutes on the first side, then carefully turn with a spatula and cook on the second side for 2–3 minutes until the sandwiches are golden brown all over and the cheese is visibly melted.

★ Remove from the skillet and cut the sandwiches in half. Let cool for a few minutes before serving and, if you wish, dunk to your heart's content in a lovely steaming bowl of tomato soup.

# BAKED BEAN TOASTIE

HERE, WE'RE GOING TO TRAVEL BACK IN TIME TO YOUR STUDENT DAYS. REMEMBER THE CHEAP, EFFECTIVE-YET-TASTY CRAP YOU ATE BACK THEN? WELL, THIS RECIPE IS BASICALLY THAT—YOU'VE COME FULL CIRCLE! ONCE YOU'VE FINISHED SOBBING SHAMEFULLY FOR EVEN CONTEMPLATING THIS RECIPE, YOU'LL NEED A BREVILLE-STYLE TOASTY MAKER. IN YOUR EMOTIONAL STATE DON'T FORGET THE CONTENTS ARE GOING TO BE HOTTER THAN THE SUN. LOSER!

2 slices white or brown bread

butter, at room temperature

a 5½-oz (150-g) can baked beans

2 tablespoons (15 g) cheese, such as Cheddar, Swiss, Provolone, or Monterey Jack, grated (optional)

a dash of Worcestershire sauce (optional)

ketchup, brown sauce, or steak sauce, to serve

**serves 1**

★ Heat the sandwich toaster. Spread one side of both slices of bread with butter, and when the sandwich toaster is hot, place the first slice, butter-side down, onto the hot plate.

★ Empty the baked beans onto the bread and top with some grated cheese and Worcestershire sauce, if using. Top with the remaining slice of bread, butter-side up, and close the sandwich toaster.

★ Toast until golden and crisp. Serve with your preferred sauce.

# PIMP MY BEANS ON TOAST

**CHEAP AND QUICK TO MAKE, BEANS ON TOAST IS THE ULTIMATE LAZY MEAL. THE BASIC VERSION IS DELICIOUS, BUT TRY THESE TWEAKS FOR SOMETHING BETTER.**

★ To make the beans on toast, put four slices of bread in the toaster, heat up a tin of baked beans on the hob or in the microwave, and pour on the toast. Simple.

★ Cheese: it should be law that grated Cheddar is included on every plate of beans.

★ Hot sauce: pour as much in as you can handle to release a rush of endorphins.

★ Mexi-beans: add pinches of chili powder, cumin, and paprika for a nod to chili con carne.

★ Indian beans: add ¼ teaspoon garam masala and/or curry powder to spice beans up a treat.

★ Eggs: A fried or poached egg with an oozing yoke blends seemlessly with beans.

4 slices thick bread

1 14-oz. (400-g) can baked beans

**additions**

Cheddar cheese, grated

hot sauce, such as Tabasco

spices, such as chili powder, cumin, paprika, garam masala, or curry powder

eggs

**serves 2**

# LAST NIGHT'S LEFTOVERS

**SOME LEFTOVER TAKEOUT FOODS SHOULD BEST BE CONSIGNED STRAIGHT TO THE BIN—WHO WANTS TO REVISIT FLACCID STRIPS OF GREASY DONAR MEAT THAT YOU WEREN'T EVEN SURE ABOUT AT 2AM AFTER NECKING EIGHT BEERS—BUT HERE ARE THREE THAT CAN BE ENJOYED THE DAY AFTER.**

★ Leftover pizza is top of many drinkers' lists as the ultimate takeout leftover. Aspiring gourmets might like to reheat slices in the oven, but the lazier amongst you should feel free to stuff the pizza straight in your face.

★ The remnants of a curry should be welcomed with open arms by hungover folk. An excellent, easy way to enjoy these morsels is to stick everything between two slices of bread.

★ While the batter on fried chicken will have gone soggy, you can peel it away, pick the meat off the bones, and use the chicken in salads or stir-fries.

anything you're lucky enough to find in the fridge

**serves... Well, that depends on how much is left**

# AVOCADO ON TOAST

THIS DISH USED TO BE INCREDIBLY EXOTIC, ONE YOU MIGHT ONLY FIND IN COSMOPOLITAN CITIES. NOWADAYS YOU SEE IT EVERYWHERE, USUALLY BEING WOLFED DOWN BY BEARDED HIPSTERS OR YOGA TYPES FRESH OUT OF A DOWNWARD DOG. DON'T LET THAT PUT YOU OFF, IT'S GREEN AND THEREFORE OBVIOUSLY GOOD FOR HANGOVERS. IT'S ALSO MORE OF AN ASSEMBLY JOB THAN A MEAL YOU HAVE TO COOK, IDEAL FIRST THING IN THE MORNING. IF YOU FANCY CHANGING IT UP, GO FOR IT. GIVE THE RECIPE A HISPANIC TWIST BY FRYING A SLICED RED ONION ALONG WITH SOME DICED CHORIZO, THEN SERVE IT ON THE MASHED AVOCADO AND TOP WITH A PERFECTLY POACHED EGG. OR DITCH THE TOMATOES AND THROW IN SOME FRIED CRISPY BACON. MUCH BETTER.

2 ripe avocados

freshly squeezed juice of ½ lime

1 tablespoon chopped fresh cilantro (coriander)

1 red chili, deseeded and finely chopped

½ tablespoon olive oil, plus extra for drizzling

sea salt and freshly ground black pepper

2 slices bread

8 cherry tomatoes, halved

**serves 2**

★ Slice the avocados in half, destone, and scoop out the flesh into a bowl.

★ Add the lime juice, cilantro (coriander), chili, and ½ tablespoon of olive oil to the bowl, then roughly mash everything together using a fork—you want a few lumps in there rather than a completely smooth paste. Season with salt and pepper to taste.

★ Toast your slices of bread and once ready spoon equal quanties of avocado mix onto each slice.

★ To finish, add the tomatoes to the plate, drizzle a little olive oil, and enjoy.

# TUNA MELT

I'VE GOT TO SAY, YOU'VE GOT A STRONGER CONSTITUTION THAN ME IF YOU CAN FACE A TUNA MELT WHILE HANGING. IF YOU CAN MANAGE TO GET IT DOWN YOUR NECK, THE DOUBLE PROTEIN WHACK FROM THE FISH AND THE CHEESE WILL HELP TO BREAK DOWN YOUR HANGOVER. BY THE WAY, ANY TYPE OF WHITE BREAD WILL DO HERE, JUST MAKE SURE THE SLICES ARE THICK.

a 7-oz. (200-g) can of tuna in water, drained

3 tablespoons mayonnaise

½ tablespoon capers, rinsed and finely chopped

2 cornichons or 1 dill pickle, finely diced, plus extra to serve

¼ red bell pepper, finely diced

1 tablespoon fresh tarragon, chopped

2 thick slices white crusty bread

4 slices cheese, such as Gruyère or Emmenthal

freshly ground black pepper

serves 2

★ Put the tuna in a bowl and flake the flesh. Add the mayonnaise, capers, cornichons or pickle, peppers, and tarragon and mix well. Season with plenty of black pepper.

★ Toast the bread on one side under a preheated broiler (grill), then turn it over and spread the tuna thickly on the uncooked side. Put 2 cheese slices on top of each piece of toast and broil for about 5 minutes until the cheese is golden and bubbling. Serve with extra pickles.

# A GOOD BACON SANDWICH

THIS HOLY GRAIL OF HANGOVER RECIPES CAN REPAIR ALL YOUR ILLS AND IS UNBELIEVABLY TASTY, BUT FOR SOMETHING SO SIMPLE IT CAN BE SURPRISINGLY HARD TO GET RIGHT. FIRSTLY, IN MY OPINION SMOKED STREAKY BACON IS THE WAY TO GO. FOR BREAD, TRY A WHITE CRUSTY BLOOMER, CUT NOT TOO THIN BUT NOT TOO THICK. YOU WANT THE BACON CRISPY, SO TAKE YOUR TIME COOKING IT, MAKING SURE IT'S NOT TOO HOT. ON THE FINISHED ARTICLE, MY PREFERRED CONDIMENTS ARE A SMEAR OF MUSTARD AND A SPLASH OF KETCHUP. AND IF YOU'RE A GREEDY BASTARD LIKE ME, ADD A FRIED EGG.

★ Broil (grill) or pan-fry your bacon on low heat, making sure you check it regularly and reposition it as necessary. It really is worth the extra effort for evenly cooked, crispy bacon.

★ If you have pan-fried the bacon, dip each piece of bread into the juices in the pan before generously buttering one slice. If you have broiled the bacon, then, well, tough luck. Immediately put all the bacon into the sandwich (don't drain the fat!) and squirt your sauce on top.

★ Add the other slice of bread, cut into your preferred portions (triangles seem to taste better!), and eat really quickly.

6 smoked (streaky) bacon slices

2 slices white bread of your choice

salted butter, at room temperature

condiments of your choice

**serves 1**

# LOX AND CREAM CHEESE BAGEL

LOX, IN CASE YOU DON'T KNOW, IS A JEWISH STYLE OF SALMON CURED IN BRINE. IF YOU DON'T HAPPEN TO LIVE NEAR A JEWISH DELI (BAD TIMES!) USE SMOKED SALMON, WHICH IS MORE READILY AVAILABLE. WITH REGARDS TO THE BAGEL, QUALITY MATTERS. IF YOU'RE LUCKY ENOUGH TO LIVE NEAR A JEWISH BAKERY SELLING FRESH BAGELS (GOOD TIMES!), THEN USE THOSE AND DON'T TOAST THEM. IN FACT, IF YOU'VE GOT A BAGEL SELLER DOWN THE ROAD, DITCH THIS RECIPE AND BUY A LOX AND CREAM CHEESE BAGEL FROM THEM. MUCH EASIER! IF, ON THE OTHER HAND, YOU'RE USING INFERIOR SUPERMARKET BAGELS, TOAST 'EM.

★ Toast the bagel halves and let them cool slightly before spreading one half with cream cheese.

★ Lay the lox (smoked salmon) slices on top and then add the capers or red onion, should you wish to do so. Top with the other half of the bagel, and serve.

1 plain white, poppy seed, or sesame seed bagel, cut in half

cream cheese

lox (smoked salmon) slices

a few capers, rinsed and patted dry, or slivers of red onion (optional)

**serves 1**

# FISH STICK SANDWICH

FISH STICKS (FINGERS) ARE AN ESSENTIAL FOOD GROUP FOR ANY HUNGRY-YET-LAZY PERSON. THEY SIT PATIENTLY IN THE FREEZER, READY TO BE DEPLOYED WHENEVER YOU REALLY CAN'T BE BOTHERED TO COOK ANYTHING ELSE. SO HUG YOUR FREEZER AND PROCURE THE BUILDING BLOCKS (FISH STICKS) FROM WITHIN. THEY ALSO WORK WELL IN THE "ORANGE DINNER" TRIUMVIRATE OF BAKED BEANS AND OVEN-COOKED FRIES, BUT WHERE THEY REALLY COME INTO THEIR OWN IS IN A SANDWICH. HERE THE DISH HAS BEEN GUSSIED UP BY PUTTING IT IN A FANCY ROLL ALONG WITH MIXED SALAD LEAVES AND A DOLLOP OF TARTARE SAUCE, BUT HONESTLY IT'S JUST AS GOOD SERVED BETWEEN TWO SLICES OF THE CHEAPEST WHITE BREAD YOU CAN FIND WITH A SQUEEZE OF TOMATO KETCHUP.

4 frozen fish sticks (fingers)

a bread roll (or 2 slices white bread)

butter, for spreading

a handful of mixed salad leaves, such as arugula (rocket) and/or romaine (cos) lettuce

tartare sauce (or other condiment of your choice)

sea salt and freshly ground black pepper

**serves 1**

★ First, choose your cooking method for the fish sticks (fingers)—oven cook or broil (grill), the choice is yours. The intructions will be on the packet so follow them—fish sticks usually take 12–15 minutes to cook from frozen. Remember to turn halway through cooking for an even, crispy coating.

★ While the fish sticks are cooking, prepare your bread roll. Slice in half and spread both sides with a good coating of butter. Add a layer of the salad leaves.

★ When the fish sticks are cooked, carefully remove from the oven or broiler and place them on the bed of salad leaves. Add a good spoonful of tartare sauce (or any other condiments you fancy), season with salt and pepper, and devour.

# STEAK SANDWICH

STEAK TAKES ABSOLUTELY NO TIME TO COOK WELL—PERFECT FOR AN INDULGENT QUICK FIX. IF YOU'RE RAVENOUS, LEAVE OUT THE ONIONS FOR SOMETHING EVEN QUICKER. OH, AND DON'T EVEN THINK OF COOKING YOUR STEAK ANYTHING MORE THAN MEDIUM. RUMP, ONGLET, OR RIBEYE ARE ALL GOOD ALTERNATIVE CUTS TO SIRLOIN.

4 tablespoons olive oil, plus extra for brushing

2 onions, thinly sliced

1½ lb. (750 g) sirloin steaks

4 small baguettes, halved lengthwise

½ cup (100 g) mayonnaise

4 oz. (100 g) watercress leaves

sea salt and freshly ground black pepper

French fries, to serve

**serves 4**

★ Heat the oil in a skillet (frying pan), add the onions, season with salt and pepper, and fry over medium heat until golden and caramelized. Set aside and keep warm.

★ Brush the steaks with olive oil and season well with salt and pepper. Preheat a griddle pan or heavy skillet and fry the steaks for 3 minutes on each side for rare, 4 minutes for medium. Let rest for 5 minutes, then slice thickly.

★ Meanwhile, lightly toast the baguettes and spread the insides liberally with mayonnaise. Fill with watercress leaves, the sliced beef, and all the juices, and top with the onions. Serve hot with French fries.

# CHIP BUTTY

IF YOU'RE AS HANGING AS YOU OUGHT TO BE TO ACTUALLY MAKE PROPER USE OF THIS BOOK, I CAN THINK OF NOTHING MORE ILL-ADVISED THAN TELLING YOU TO GO USE A DEEP-FAT FRYER OR GET A CHIP PAN ON THE HOB—YOU'LL MELT YOUR FRIGGING ARMS OFF! INSTEAD, STAY IN BED AND GET A TRUSTED LOVED ONE TO MAKE YOU A CHIP BUTTY USING THE BELOW RECIPE, OR PERHAPS USING OVEN CHIPS (LET'S PRETEND I DIDN'T SAY THAT). I THINK THE KEY TO A GOOD CHIP BUTTY IS DECENT FRESH WHITE BREAD, SLATHERED WITH BUTTER, AND SCALDING HOT SALTY CHIPS. EASY.

---

1 lb. (450 g) Maris Piper or Russet potatoes

vegetable oil, for frying

sea salt and malt vinegar, to taste

2 white rolls, split open

butter, for spreading

sauce of your choice, to serve

**serves 2**

---

★ Peel the potatoes and cut them lengthwise into slices that are about ½ in. (1 cm) thick. Cut these slices into chips. Put the chips into a bowl of cold water and let soak for a couple of hours if possible. If time is short, rinse well under plenty of cold water. This process removes extra starch. Drain and pat the chips dry.

★ Pour some vegetable oil for deep-frying into a deep frying pan or an electric deep-fat fryer and heat to 350°F (180°C), then fry the chips until crisp and golden. Drain on paper towels.

★ Add salt and vinegar to the chips, then pile into the split buttered rolls. Serve with a good squirt of your sauce of choice. Eat immediately.

# QUICK THAI CHICKEN CURRY

I CAN'T SAY A PROPER CURRY IS SOMETHING I'D COOK TO REPAIR MY DRUNK SELF AFTER A NIGHT OUT. IF I EVER DID MAKE A THAI CURRY TO SORT MYSELF OUT, THEN IT'D BE A QUICK ONE, AND THIS DEFINITELY IS. AS YOU'VE GOT A CHOICE OF WHICH VEGETABLES YOU SLING IN, I SUGGEST GETTING THE BIGGEST VITAMIN PUNCH YOU CAN MANAGE BY USING A VARIETY OF COLORED VEG. EAT THE RAINBOW, PEOPLE!

scant 1 cup (200 g) Thai jasmine or fragrant rice

1 14-oz. (400-ml) can coconut milk

3 tablespoons (50 g) green Thai curry paste

1 tablespoon sunflower oil

14 oz. (400 g) chicken breast, cut into bite-sized pieces

½ teaspoon kaffir lime leaf purée

1 teaspoon Thai fish sauce

scant 1 cup (100 g) mixed fresh vegetables of your choice

a handful of Thai sweet basil leaves

**serves 2**

★ Cook the rice according to the packet instructions.

★ Meanwhile, pour the coconut milk into a saucepan and gently bring it to near boiling. Remove from the heat and stir in the Thai curry paste. Set aside.

★ Heat the oil into a large skillet (frying pan) or wok and stir fry the chicken pieces over high heat for 2 minutes, or until golden.

★ Pour the warm, spiced coconut milk over the fried chicken pieces and add the kaffir lime leaf purée and fish sauce. Add any vegetables you are using at this stage. Stir and simmer gently for about 12 minutes, or until everything is cooked through.

★ Divide the curry between warmed serving bowls, scatter over the basil leaves, and serve immediately with a bowl of rice on the side.

# CHAPTER 4

# HEALTHY AND (PSEUDO) SCIENTIFIC MEALS

## BIRCHER MUESLI

IF YOU'RE THE TYPE WHO DEALS WITH A HANGOVER BY SUBJECTING YOURSELF TO A TORTUOUS COLD SHOWER, 50 PRESS-UPS, AND A 10K RUN, THEN THIS ONE'S FOR YOU. TO BE FAIR, IT'S TASTY AND CONTAINS LOADS OF STUFF THAT'S GOOD FOR YOU, BUT THE SOGGY TEXTURE ISN'T FOR SOME. PREPARE IT A FEW DAYS IN ADVANCE AND STORE IN THE FRIDGE, BUT OMIT THE APPLE UNTIL THE END, OTHERWISE IT'LL GO BROWN.

1 cup (125 g) rolled oats

½ cup (75 g) (golden) raisins

¾ cup (175 ml) apple juice

freshly squeezed juice of 1 lemon

¼ cup (100 g) plain yogurt

1 apple, cored, peeled, and grated

3 tablespoons slivered (flaked) almonds

mixed summer berries, to serve

clear honey, to serve

**serves 4–6**

★ Put the oats and raisins in a large dish. Pour over the apple and lemon juices. Cover with a dish cloth and let soak overnight. Alternatively, place in an airtight container and refrigerate, especially if it is very hot.

★ The next morning when you're ready for breakfast, stir the yogurt, apple, and almonds into the soaked muesli. Divide between 4–6 bowls, scatter some brightly colored berries over the top, and finish with a zigzag of honey.

# PORRIDGE WITH APPLES AND BLACKBERRIES

GOOD OLD PORRIDGE, GREAT FOR FILLING YOU UP, EASILY DIGESTIBLE WHEN YOU'VE HAD ONE TOO MANY, SIMPLE TO MAKE, CHEAP AS CHIPS, AND ABSOLUTELY DELICIOUS WHEN IT'S MADE RIGHT. IT'S A HANGOVER SUPERFOOD, PEOPLE! EVERYONE LIKES IT PREPARED DIFFERENTLY, BUT PERSONALLY I RECKON HALF MILK, HALF WATER IS THE WAY TO GO. ADD A PINCH OF SALT TOO; IT MAY SOUND STRANGE WHEN YOU'RE MAKING IT SWEET, BUT IT DEFINITELY ADDS SOMETHING. FINALLY, A BLOB OF GREEK YOGURT WON'T HURT AT ALL.

★ Put the oats in a saucepan and add the milk and 1 cup (250 ml) water. Add a pinch of salt, cover with a lid, and slowly bring to the boil over medium heat. Once the mixture is bubbling, turn the heat to low, add the raisins, and cook for 2–3 minutes, stirring occasionally. The porridge should be thick and creamy. Take off the heat and let stand with a lid on for 2–3 minutes while you cook the apples.

★ Put the butter in a frying pan over high heat until the bubbling subsides. Stir in the apples, sugar, and cinnamon. Let caramelize for 2–3 minutes, then flip the apple wedges over so the other side gets a chance to become golden too. Finally, add the blackberries and heat for a couple of minutes just so they warm through a little.

★ Meanwhile, spoon the porridge into 4 bowls and stir in a little cold milk to stop it becoming too thick. Spoon the caramelized apples and blackberries on top and serve straightaway.

¾ cup (100 g) rolled oats

1 cup (250 ml) whole milk, plus a little extra to thin

a pinch of salt

½ cup (75 g) (golden) raisins

1 tablespoon butter

2 apples, cored and cut into slim wedges

3 tablespoons demerara sugar

a pinch of ground cinnamon

1 cup (100 g) blackberries

**serves 4**

# FRUITY QUINOA AND BEAN STEW

DESPITE BEING IMPOSSIBLE TO PRONOUNCE, QUINOA IS A BIT TRENDY RIGHT NOW, BEING A SUPERFOOD THAT'S HIGH IN PROTEIN, CALCIUM, IRON, AND ALL THAT. WHEN COMBINED, AS IT IS HERE, WITH BEANS AND DRIED FRUIT YOU'VE GOT A SUPERB HANGOVER RECOVERY MEAL. JUST FOR PRACTICALITY, MAKE THIS THE DAY BEFORE AND THEN WHEN YOU DO ROLL OUT OF YOUR PIT AT 4PM, ALL YOU'VE GOT TO DO IS REHEAT IT AND MAKE SOME COUSCOUS. LET'S FACE IT, THAT'S ABOUT ALL YOU'LL BE GOOD FOR.

★ Rinse the lentils and quinoa and put them in a saucepan of boiling water. Reduce the heat to a gentle simmer and add the Baharat spice blend. Cook, uncovered, for 20 minutes, or until thick. Drain well.

★ Heat the oil in a stovetop casserole dish and gently fry the onions and garlic until softened but not brown. Add the chopped tomatoes and the cooked lentils and quinoa. Stir well. Add the vegetable stock and bring back to a simmer.

★ Add the hot sauce, bay leaves, thyme, apricots, raisins, chilis, mixed beans, chickpeas, and peppers. Stir well. Bring to the boil, then reduce the heat to a very gentle simmer and cook, covered, for at least 1 hour. Stir occasionally.

★ Add more stock if it looks dry, but allow the sauce to thicken. Taste and season with salt and pepper. Serve with couscous.

1 cup (200 g) red split lentils

⅔ cup (100 g) quinoa

1 teaspoon Baharat spice blend or Ras el Hanout

1 tablespoon olive oil

2 onions, chopped

6 garlic cloves, crushed

2 14-oz. (400-g) cans chopped tomatoes

2½ cups (600 ml) good vegetable stock

3 tablespoons hot sauce

2 bay leaves

1 sprig of fresh thyme

½ cup (75 g) chopped dried apricots

½ cup (75 g) (golden) raisins

1–2 fresh red chilis, chopped

2 14-oz. (400-g) cans mixed beans, drained

1 14-oz. (400-g) can chickpeas (aka garbanzo beans), drained

2 red bell peppers, deseeded and sliced

sea salt and freshly ground black pepper

cooked couscous, to serve

**serves 8**

# CAESAR SALAD

CREATED IN 1924 BY ITALIAN RESTAURATEUR CAESAR CARDINI (NOT IN 50 BC BY JULIUS CAESAR, YOU HUNGOVER FOOLS!), THIS CLASSIC IS FULL OF TASTY INGREDIENTS. THE BACON AND AVOCADO VARIATION IS MY TIP FOR SORTING OUT YOUR SORE HEAD.

★ Cut the crusts off the bread and discard. Cut the bread into cubes. Heat the olive oil in a skillet (frying pan), add the bread cubes, and cook until golden brown. Set aside.

★ To make the classic Caesar dressing, put the egg in a small saucepan and cover with warm water. Bring to just simmering, turn off the heat, and leave the egg for 2 minutes. Run under cold water to stop the egg cooking further.

★ Crack the egg into a large serving bowl and whisk in the garlic, mustard, Worcestershire sauce, salt, pepper, vinegar, lemon juice, and anchovies. Slowly whisk in the extra virgin olive oil.

★ Add the lettuce and toss well, then scatter over the Parmesan cheese and croûtons to serve.

## Variations

**Chicken Caesar:** Roast 3–4 chicken breasts until golden and cooked through. Let cool, then slice and add to the salad.

**Bacon and avocado Caesar:** Fry 8 slices of bacon until crisp. Chop and add to the salad with 1 sliced avocado.

**Anchovy and poached egg Caesar:** For a more intense anchovy flavor, toss whole, mild, good-quality anchovy fillets through the salad. Top each salad with a poached egg to serve.

2 thick slices dense white bread

2 tablespoons olive oil

1 large or 3 baby romaine (cos) lettuce

½ cup (40 g) shaved Parmesan

**classic Caesar dressing**

1 fresh egg, at room temperature

1 small garlic clove, crushed

1 teaspoon Dijon mustard

1 teaspoon Worcestershire sauce

¼ teaspoon sea salt

⅛ teaspoon freshly ground black pepper

1 tablespoon white wine vinegar

1 tablespoon freshly squeezed lemon juice

2 anchovy fillets, finely chopped

4 tablespoons extra virgin olive oil

**serves 4**

# RED SALAD with beets, red cabbage, and harissa dressing

BELIEVE IT OR NOT, BEETS (BEETROOT) ARE FANTASTIC FOR HANGOVERS. THEY CONTAIN BETA CYANIN (THE PIGMENT THAT GIVES BEETS THE RED COLOR), WHICH IS AN ANTIOXIDANT THAT SPEEDS UP DETOXIFICATION IN YOUR LIVER. WINNER! SO AS WELL AS THAT DOING THE JOB, I RECKON THE FRESH CHILIS AND THE SPICY HARISSA DRESSING OUGHT TO GIVE YOUR BODY A MUCH NEEDED KICK IN THE ASS, TOO.

6–8 small beets (beetroot)

2–4 small whole heads of garlic

olive oil, for roasting

1 small red cabbage

2 tablespoons white wine vinegar, cider vinegar, or lemon juice

2 red onions, very finely sliced

1 tablespoon red wine vinegar mixed with a pinch of salt

sea salt and freshly ground black pepper

2 medium red chilis, finely sliced

**harissa dressing**

½ cup (125 ml) extra virgin olive oil

1 tablespoon harissa paste

**serves 4–6**

★ Preheat the oven to 400°F (200°C) Gas 6.

★ Leave the beets (beetroot) whole and unpeeled. Cut the top off each garlic, about ½ in. (1 cm) from the stalk. Put the beets and garlic in a small baking dish, add olive oil, turn to coat, then season with salt and pepper. Roast in the preheated oven for about 30–45 minutes or until the beets and garlic are tender (you may have to remove the beets first). When cooked, remove from the oven and cut the beets into 4 wedges.

★ About 15 minutes before the beets are cooked, cut the cabbage in quarters and remove the white cores. Cut the quarters into fine slices and put in a bowl. Sprinkle with vinegar and turn and mash the cabbage with your hands. Put the sliced onion in a bowl and cover with boiling water. Drain just before using.

★ Push the roasted pulp out of 4 garlic cloves and put it in a serving bowl. Add the oil and harissa and beat with a fork. Drain the onions, pat dry with paper towels, then add to the bowl. Sprinkle with the red wine vinegar and salt mix. Add the cabbage and beets and toss gently. Taste and adjust the seasoning with salt and pepper and top with the chilis. Put the heads of garlic beside for people to press out the delicious flesh themselves.

# CABBAGE SOUP

THIS ISN'T A STITCH-UP TO GET YOU NECKING GALLONS OF CABBAGE SOUP, OH NO. IN FACT, CABBAGE HAS BEEN USED AS A HANGOVER REMEDY AS FAR BACK AS ANCIENT GREECE. APPARENTLY, ONE OF THE BY-PRODUCTS OF A NIGHT ON THE SAUCE ARE TOXINS CALLED COGENERS AND CABBAGE HELPS TO ERADICATE THEM. PROBABLY THE BEST WAY TO GET THE GREEN STUFF DOWN YOU SO IT CAN GET TO WORK IS IN THE FORM OF THIS SIMPLE SOUP. ON THE PLUS SIDE, IT'LL SOOTHE BOTH YOUR HEADACHE AND NAUSEA. AND THE INEVITABLE NEGATIVE? FLATULENCE. YOU'LL BE EXTREMELY UNPLEASANT TO BE AROUND AND WILL HAVE TO TAKE CARE NOT TO EXPEL YOUR INNARDS WITH THE VIOLENT FARTING. HOLD ON TIGHT!

2 onions, sliced

1 tablespoon butter

7 cups (1.7 liters) vegetable stock

½ head green cabbage

1 14-oz. (400-g) can chopped tomatoes

1 tablespoon cider vinegar

2 carrots, chopped

1 turnip, cubed

1 potato, peeled and cubed

sea salt, freshly ground black pepper, and chopped parsley, to season

**serves 6–8**

★ Fry the onions in the butter until tender.

★ Add the stock, cabbage, tomatoes, and vinegar. Heat until it boils.

★ Now reduce the heat and simmer uncovered for 30 minutes. Add the carrots, turnip, and potato and simmer for a further 15 minutes. Season with salt, pepper, and parsley. Be prepared for the ensuing monstrous flatulence.

HEALTHY AND (PSEUDO) SCIENTIFIC MEALS

# TOMATO, AVOCADO, AND LIME SALAD
## with crisp tortillas

LOADS OF GOOD STUFF HERE FOR A HANGOVER. TOMATOES ARE FULL OF VITAMINS AND THE ANTIOXIDANT LYCOPENE; AVOCADOS ARE HIGH IN PROTEIN AND PACKED WITH POTASSIUM. AS ALL SAILORS WILL TELL YOU, LIMES WILL STOP YOU GETTING SCURVY AND THAT'S SOMETHING YOU REALLY DON'T NEED ON TOP OF A HANGOVER. BASICALLY, EAT THIS SALAD.

★ Put the lime juice in a bowl. Cut the avocados in half, remove the stones, and peel. Cut each half into 4 wedges and toss with the lime juice.

★ Using a small knife, cut the top and bottom off of the whole lime. Cut away the skin and pith. Carefully slice between each segment and remove the flesh. Combine the lime flesh with the avocados, cilantro (coriander), tomatoes, and 4 tablespoons of the oil. Season to taste with salt and pepper and set aside.

★ Preheat the broiler (grill) to hot.

★ In a small bowl, combine the garlic and remaining 2 tablespoons of oil. Brush the oil and garlic mixture over the tortillas and toast under the preheated broiler for about 1 minute until brown.

★ Break the toasted tortillas into pieces and scatter over the salad just before serving.

---

freshly squeezed juice of 1 lime, plus 1 whole lime

4 ripe avocados

a large bunch of fresh cilantro (coriander), leaves only

24 small tomatoes, halved

6 tablespoons olive oil

2 garlic cloves, crushed

2 soft flour tortillas

sea salt and freshly ground black pepper

**serves 6**

# NEW POTATO, CRISP SALAMI, AND SESAME SALAD

PERHAPS MORE OF A PREVENTATIVE MEASURE THAN A CURE, THIS ONE. THERE IS SOME EVIDENCE TO SUGGEST THAT EATING FATTY, BUTTERY FOODS BEFORE A HEAVY BOUT OF DRINKING MAY SLOW DOWN HOW QUICKLY YOU GET DRUNK AND THEREFORE COULD MEAN A MILDER HANGOVER. THE POTATOES, SALAMI, AND MAYONNAISE IN THIS RECIPE CERTAINLY HAVE THE REQUIRED ATTRIBUTES. GIVE THIS A GO BEFORE HEADING OUT ON THE TOWN AND SEE IF IT WORKS. IF NOTHING ELSE, IT'S VERY TASTY.

**lemon mayonnaise**

1 egg yolk, at room temperature

2 tablespoons freshly squeezed lemon juice

a pinch of sea salt

½ cup (125 ml) plain-flavored oil, such as grape seed

1 teaspoon sesame oil

1¾ lb. (800 g) waxy new potatoes

a pinch of sea salt

2 tablespoons sesame seeds

6 oz. (150 g) thinly sliced salami (a fatty, unflavored variety)

½ quantity lemon mayonnaise (see above)

3 oz. (75 g) arugula (rocket)

a small bunch of dill, chopped

**serves 6**

★ To make the lemon mayonnaise, put the egg yolk, half the lemon juice, and salt in a bowl. Whisk to mix. While whisking continuously, slowly add the plain-flavored oil a drop at a time until fully incorporated. Whisk in the sesame oil and remaining lemon juice. Cover and set aside until needed. (Note that this recipe makes approximately double the quantity required for this salad. The remainder will keep in the refrigerator for up to 3 days.)

★ If necessary, cut the potatoes into even-sized pieces. Put in a large saucepan. Cover with cold water, add the salt, bring to the boil, then simmer until tender. Drain and set aside.

★ Heat a skillet (frying pan) to medium heat, add the sesame seeds, and toast for about 6–8 minutes, stirring until golden. Set aside.

★ Reheat the skillet until hot, add the salami slices, and cook for a few minutes on each side until browned. Remove and drain on paper towels. (It will crisp up more as it cools.)

★ Arrange the arugula (rocket) in a serving bowl. Toss the potatoes with the lemon mayonnaise and pile on top of the arugula. Scatter with half the toasted sesame seeds and dill. Crumble over the crisp salami and scatter with the remaining sesame seeds and dill to serve.

# ROASTED VEGETABLE SOUP

A PERFECT RECOVERY AID WHEN YOU'RE PROPERLY FLAT OUT FROM OVERINDULGENCE; THE TOMATOES AND THE THYME ESPECIALLY ARE EXACTLY WHAT YOU NEED TO SORT YOU OUT. SOUPS ALMOST ALWAYS TASTE BETTER WHEN THEY'VE HAD TIME TO SETTLE, SO MAKE THIS THE DAY BEFORE AND WARM IT UP IN THE MICROWAVE.

2 lb. (700 g) plum tomatoes; halved

1 red onion, finely chopped

2 carrots, finely chopped

1 small red chili

2 garlic cloves, peeled

a few fresh thyme or rosemary sprigs

2 tablespoons olive oil

1⅓ cups (350 ml) passata (if unable to find use chopped tomatoes)

½ teaspoon sugar

a squeeze of fresh lime juice

sea salt and freshly ground black pepper

a handful of fresh cilantro (coriander), roughly chopped

a drizzle of extra virgin olive oil and warm crusty bread, to serve

**serves 2–4**

★ Preheat the oven to 400°F (200°C) Gas 6.

★ Put the plum tomatoes, onion, and carrots in a roasting pan. Add the chili, garlic, thyme or rosemary sprigs, and olive oil and toss until the vegetables are well coated in the oil. Place in the preheated oven and roast for about 25 minutes, turning the vegetables occasionally using a large spoon.

★ Remove from the oven and discard the chili. Blend the roasted vegetables, garlic, and herbs with the passata to the desired consistency in a blender. Add the sugar, lime juice, and ⅔ cup (150 ml) cold water, and season well with salt and pepper.

★ Pour the mixture into a large pan and gently heat through. Add the chopped coriander just before serving. Ladle into warmed serving bowls and drizzle with a little extra virgin olive oil. Serve immediately with warm crusty bread.

# SPICY RED PEPPER AND TOMATO SOUP

HERE'S ANOTHER EASILY DIGESTIBLE AND EXTREMELY GOOD FOR YOU SOUP RECIPE CONTAINING ACE THINGS TO GET YOU UP ON YOUR FEET. THE STAR INGREDIENT HERE IS THE CRISPY BACON SLICES—I CAN'T STRESS ENOUGH HOW VITAL BACON IS TO FIX A HANGOVER, SO PILE LOADS ON.

6 medium red bell peppers, roughly chopped

1 lb. (450 g) carrots, roughly chopped

1–2 red chilis, deseeded and halved

1½ lb. (700 g) ripe plum tomatoes

3 large garlic cloves, peeled

6 tablespoons olive oil

2 teaspoons smoked sweet paprika

5 cups (1.25 liters) vegetable or beef stock

sea salt and freshly ground black pepper

crisply fried bacon slices, to serve

**serves 8**

★ Preheat the oven to 400°F (200°C) Gas 6.

★ Put the peppers, carrots, chilis, tomatoes, and garlic in a large roasting pan, then toss them in the oil. Season well and roast in the preheated oven for about 30 minutes until all the vegetables are soft and slightly charred at the edges.

★ Transfer half the vegetables to a blender, add the paprika and half the stock, and blitz until smooth. Pour into a saucepan and repeat with the remaining vegetables and stock, adding extra stock if it seems too thick. Reheat until almost boiling, add salt and pepper to taste, then serve with the bacon on top.

# COUSCOUS SALAD

## with feta, peas, and spring beans

CHEAP, CARB HEAVY, FILLING, QUICK, INOFFENSIVE, BELOVED OF HEALTH-FOOD NUTS AND
MOROCCANS; I GIVE YOU COUSCOUS. A BIG BOWL OF THIS, FULL OF VEG AND TOPPED WITH SALTY
FETA, WILL HELP OVERCOME LAST NIGHT'S EXCESSES. IF YOU CAN MANAGE TO CHANGE YOUR
EXPRESSION FROM A FIXED GRIMACE, PULL A SMUG FACE AS YOU MUNCH AWAY—YOU DESERVE IT.

1½ cups (270 g) couscous

1⅔ cups (400 ml) boiling water

5 tablespoons olive oil

1 garlic clove, crushed

3 scallions (spring onions), thinly sliced

2 tablespoons fresh dill, chopped

2 tablespoons fresh chives, chopped

1 tablespoon lemon zest

1 tablespoon lemon flesh, chopped

2 cups (250 g) chopped feta

1 cup (150 g) sugar snap peas

1 cup (150 g) frozen fava (broad) beans, defrosted

1 cup (150 g) frozen peas, defrosted

freshly ground black pepper

**serves 4**

★ Put the couscous in a large bowl and pour over the boiling water. Cover with plastic wrap (clingfilm) or a plate and leave to swell for 10 minutes.

★ Pour the olive oil into a mixing bowl and add the garlic, scallions (spring onions), dill, chives, lemon zest and flesh, and season with black pepper. Add the feta, turn in the oil, and set aside while you cook the beans.

★ Bring a medium saucepan of unsalted water to the boil. Add the sugar snap peas, bring back to the boil, and cook for 1 minute. Add the fava (broad) beans, bring back to the boil, and cook for 1 minute. Finally, add the peas and cook for 2 minutes. Drain.

★ Uncover the couscous and stir in the hot beans and peas. Transfer to serving bowls and top with the feta, spooning over the flavored oil as you go. Stir well before serving.

# CHAPTER 5

# HAIR OF THE DOG COCKTAILS

## CORPSE REVIVER

THIS ONE'S FOR WHEN YOU'VE GONE BALLS TO THE WALL MAD ON BOOZE BUT NOW FEEL LIKE YOU'RE HANGING ON TO LIFE BY A THREAD—IT'LL EITHER END YOUR AGONY OR MAKE YOU FEEL WORSE. YOU PAYS YOUR MONEY AND YOU TAKES YOUR CHANCES.

★ Add all the ingredients to a shaker filled with ice. Shake and strain into a frosted martini glass. Garnish with an orange zest and serve.

1 oz. (25 ml) calvados

1 oz. (25 ml) sweet vermouth

1 oz. (25 ml) brandy

orange zest, to garnish

**serves 1**

## VODKA ESPRESSO

SO YOU'RE CLUTCHING YOUR HEAD, WHIMPERING THAT YOU'LL NEVER DRINK AGAIN. BUT OF COURSE YOU WILL—WE ALL DO—SO WHY NOT MAN UP AND TAKE THE EDGE OFF WITH THIS COFFEE AND VODKA COMBINATION. IT'S EXACTLY WHAT YOU NEED TO SIMULTANEOUSLY WAKE YOU UP AND CALM YOU DOWN… ERRR… OR MAKE YOU VOMIT COPIOUSLY.

1 oz. (25 ml) espresso coffee

2 oz. (50 ml) vodka

a dash of sugar syrup, to taste

3 coffee beans, to garnish

**serves 1**

★ Pour the espresso coffee into a shaker, add the vodka and sugar syrup to taste. Shake the mixture sharply and strain into an old-fashioned glass filled with ice. Garnish with three coffee beans.

# BLOODY MARY

4 cups (1 liter) tomato juice

1 lemon

1–2 tablespoons Worcestershire sauce, to taste

½ cup (125 ml) vodka

a pinch of celery salt

sea salt and freshly ground black pepper

Tabasco sauce, to taste

**serves 4–6**

AN ABSOLUTE BLOODY "AHEM" CLASSIC AND A PERSONAL FAVORITE. DRINK ONE (OR IF YOU'RE PARTICULARLY PARCHED, TWO) OF THESE AND IT'LL FIX YOU STRAIGHT UP WHEN YOU'RE A BLEARY-EYED MESS, GETTING YOU IN THE MOOD FOR A BIT OF FOOD. IF, LIKE ME, YOU WANT IT *SCORCHIO*, ADD A FEW EXTRA SPLASHES OF TABASCO OR EVEN SOME GRATED HORSERADISH… OR PERHAPS BOTH! MENTAL.

★ Mix all the ingredients together in a pitcher (jug). Taste and adjust the seasonings if necessary, adding more heat, pepper, or lime as you wish.

★ Add a couple of handfuls of ice to the pitcher and serve with a stack of tumblers.

# MULLED MARY

A HOT VERSION OF THE ABOVE THAT'S PERFECT FOR HUNGOVER WINTER MORNINGS WHEN YOUR BODY CRAVES HEAT, TOMATO, AND VODKA (OBVIOUSLY), BUT CAN'T BEAR THE THOUGHT OF ANYTHING COLD. YOU CAN RAMP UP THE WARMTH FACTOR WITH SOME EXTRA TABASCO AS WELL. I CONSIDER THIS DRINK THE PERFECT JUMP-START OVER THE CHRISTMAS PERIOD. JOYEUX NOEL INDEED!

★ Using the same ingredient as above, put the tomato juice in a saucepan. Cut half the lemon into slices and squeeze the juice from the remaining half into the pan.

★ Add the lemon slices, Worcestershire sauce, and some salt and pepper to taste. Bring slowly to the boil and simmer gently, uncovered, for 10 minutes.

★ Remove the pan from the heat and let cool for about 20 minutes. Stir in the vodka and add celery salt to taste. Serve immediately.

# BOILERMAKER

A BOILERMAKER IS THE GO-TO HAIR OF THE DOG CHOICE FOR LUNATIC BOOZERS AND BORDERLINE ALCOHOLICS EVERYWHERE (WHO, ME?). IT'S ALSO REMARKABLY SIMPLE: A SHOT OF WHISKEY WITH A BEER ON THE SIDE; THAT'S IT. BELOW YOU HAVE 3 DIFFERENT OPTIONS ON HOW TO GET IT DOWN YOUR NECK.

★ Choose one of the following:
1) Shoot the whiskey (American is best) and drink the beer as a chaser.
2) Drop the shot into the beer, bomb style.
3) Sip some beer from the bottle, then top it up with the whiskey.

★ If whiskey isn't your bag, you could try tequila paired with a light Mexican beer or go Jamaican style with a Steel Bottom—a shot of Wray & Nephew overproof rum washed down with a bottle of Red Stripe.

> 1 oz. (25 ml) whiskey
>
> 1 bottle of pale ale or beer of your choice
>
> **serves 1**

# PICKLEBACK

AS A CONCEPT, THE PICKLEBACK SOUNDS AWFUL: NECKING A SHOT OF WHISKEY FOLLOWED BY A SHOT OF PICKLE BRINE. HARD TO BELIEVE, BUT IT'S ACTUALLY AWESOME. THE ROUGH BURN OF THE WHISKEY IS INSTANTLY NEUTRALIZED BY THE SALTY, SWEET-AND-SOUR BRINE. IT'S A SUPERB WAY TO GET BOOZED. I'M NOT ENTIRELY SURE IF PICKLE JUICE IS THE BEST IDEA WHEN HUNGOVER, BUT THEN IF YOU HAD ANY REAL COMMON SENSE YOU PROBABLY WOULDN'T BE READING THIS AT ALL.

★ Pour the two liquids into separate glasses. Drink the whiskey, then the pickle brine. Simple.

★ A slice of pickle makes an excellent third stage to the ritual. Other spirits can also be used, but I recommend Jameson's Irish whiskey or bourbon.

> 1 oz. (25 ml) whiskey
>
> 1 oz. (25 ml) pickle brine
>
> **serves 1**

# MIMOSA

WHEN YOU NEED A VITAMIN C BOOST FROM ORANGE JUICE, BUT CAN'T FACE NECKING SOMETHING SO HEALTHY, JUST MIX IT WITH YOUR CHOICE OF SPARKLING WINE. PERFECTO! DEPENDING ON THE CIRCLES YOU MOVE IN THERE'S SOME POTENTIAL FOR SOCIAL SUICIDE HERE, SO BE WARY. FRESHLY SQUEEZED BLOOD ORANGE JUICE TOPPED WITH VINTAGE CHAMPAGNE; YES. SUNNY DELIGHT TOPPED UP WITH LAMBRINI; NO.

6 blood or ordinary oranges
1 bottle sparkling wine, chilled
6 small chunks of peach (optional)

**serves 6**

★ Squeeze the oranges and divide the juice between 6 glasses. Top up with wine and serve. If you're feeling fancy, add a chunk of peach to the bottom of the glass to make a half-assed attempt at a bellini.

# COOKIES AND IRISH CREAM

IF YOU HAVE THE PALATE OF A CHILD PLUS THE BATTERED LIVER OF A CHRONIC BOOZER, THIS MILKSHAKE IS JUST THE TICKET. IT'S APPALLINGLY SWEET BUT SHOT THROUGH WITH LOVELY ALCOHOL. BOOM! FOR LAZIER BOOZERS, JUST EAT ICE CREAM FROM THE TUB ACCOMPANIED BY SWIGS OF BAILEYS STRAIGHT FROM THE BOTTLE. STAY CLASSY.

7 oz. (200 ml) Irish cream liqueur, such as Baileys

⅔ cup (150 ml) whole milk

8 scoops vanilla ice cream

8 chocolate sandwich cookies, such as Oreo, plus 2, to serve

2 milkshake glasses

**serves 2**

★ Place the glasses in the freezer to chill for a few minutes.

★ Put all of the ingredients (except for the cookies used for garnishing the glasses) in a blender and pulse until smooth and thick.

★ Divide the milkshake between the chilled glasses and edge each glass with a cookie—scrape some of the filling out of one half of each cookie and hook over the side of the glass like a lime wedge.

# THE ELVIS

I LOVE THIS; A MILKSHAKE BASED ON THE INFAMOUS "ELVIS" SANDWICH—FRIED BANANA, PEANUT BUTTER, AND BACON. THIS IMPROBABLE YET UNDENIABLY TASTY COMBO WAS A FAVORITE OF "THE KING" AND, TO BE FAIR, PROBABLY CONTRIBUTED TO HIS UNTIMELY DEMISE. DON'T LET THAT PUT YOU OFF, AS A HAIR-OF-THE-DOG OFFERING IT'S SUPERB. THE ORIGINAL RECIPE LEAVES OUT THE BACON, BUT I SUGGEST PUTTING IT IN ANYWAY—CRISP, STREAKY, MAYBE SWEETENED WITH MAPLE SYRUP, BROKEN UP, AND SCATTERED ON TOP AS A GARNISH.

½ cup (60 g) chocolate shavings, plus extra to serve

2¾ oz. (80 ml) crème de banane, plus extra for the glasses

4 scoops peanut butter ice cream

1 oz. (30 ml) vanilla vodka

1 large banana, peeled and roughly chopped

⅓ cup (100 ml) whole milk

canned whipped cream

2 milkshake glasses

**serves 2**

★ Place the glasses in the freezer to chill for a few minutes. Once chilled, decorate the glasses with chocolate. Place the shavings in a shallow bowl wide enough to fit the glasses. Coat the rim of each glass with crème de banane before upturning them into the chocolate. Twist to coat the rims, then set aside.

★ Place all the ingredients except for the cream and extra chocolate shavings in a blender and pulse until smooth and thick. Divide between the glasses and top with a squirt of cream and a sprinkling of chocolate shavings. Thank you very much!

# HOT TODDY

THIS TODDY IS ABOUT AS MEDICINAL AS IT GETS. NOT ONLY WILL IT HELP YOUR HANGOVER, THE WARMING BLEND OF SPICES, HONEY, LEMON, AND WHISKEY WILL SOOTHE ALMOST ANY ACHES AND PAINS YOU CARE TO THROW AT IT. IT'S ALSO VERY WELCOME ON A COLD WINTER DAY. STICK SOME IN A THERMOS WHEN YOU'RE OUT AND FREEZING YOUR BALLS OFF. NO ONE WILL THINK YOU'VE GOT A DRINK PROBLEM (MUCH) WHEN YOU'RE SWIGGING AT YOUR "MEDICINE," I PROMISE.

5 cloves

2 lemon slices

2 oz. (50 ml) whiskey

1 oz. (25 ml) freshly squeezed lemon juice

2 teaspoons clear honey or sugar syrup, to taste

⅓ cup (80 ml) just-boiled water

1 cinnamon stick, to serve (optional)

**serves 1**

★ Skewer the cloves into the lemon slices and put them in a heatproof glass.

★ Add the whiskey, lemon juice, and honey or sugar syrup to taste.

★ Top up with boiling water and add a cinnamon stick, if using. Serve immediately.

# PRAIRIE OYSTER

ONE FOR THE TRUE HANGOVER SADISTS, THE PRAIRIE OYSTER IS BASICALLY A RAW EGG YOLK WITH A FEW EXTRAS TO MAKE IT MORE PALATABLE. EVERYBODY SHOULD TRY THIS AT LEAST ONCE, THEN NEVER AGAIN.

a dash of olive oil

1 egg yolk

a dash of Tabasco sauce

2 dashes of Worcestershire sauce

2 dashes of vinegar or lemon juice

salt and pepper

**serves 1**

★ Rinse a martini glass with the olive oil and carefully add the egg yolk. Add the seasoning to taste and serve.

★ Hold your breath and down it in one. As you feel it slide down your neck, you'll soon realize why it's called an oyster.

★ P.G. Wodehouse's famous butler, Jeeves, was a big fan of raw eggs and hot sauce after a rough night. In fact, the morning they first ever met, Jeeves' initial service to his new master was to mix him up a variant of the prairie oyster.

★ The original prairie oyster— favored by cowboys on the prairies of North America— featured very different ingredients indeed. Instead of the raw egg, they opted for fried bull's testicles. Here's a bit of free advice: stick with the egg version. Whatever route you go down, *ouef* or classic gonad flavor, I suggest getting it down in one.

# FERNET

IF ANY LIQUEUR COULD BE CALLED A CULT CLASSIC, FERNET BRANCA—FAVORED BY HIP BARTENDERS AND LUNATIC BOOZEHOUNDS— IS IT. THE TASTE IS ALMOST INDESCRIBABLE: BITTER AND HERBAL WITH A ROUGH COUGH MEDICINE VIBE. IT'S NOT EXACTLY PLEASANT, BUT IS AN ACQUIRED TASTE, SO KEEP AT IT AND BE REWARDED WITH ITS FAMOUS (UNPROVEN) MEDICINAL QUALITIES, WHICH INCLUDE TREATING CHOLERA (USEFUL!), COLIC, MENSTRUAL PAIN, AND HANGOVERS—WINNER!

1 tablespoon Fernet Branca
1 tablespoon sweet vermouth
2 oz. (50 ml) gin
cocktail cherry

**serves 1**

★ Simply mix the Fernet, vermouth, and gin with ice and strain into a cocktail glass. Add a cocktail cherry for a token bit of vitamin C.

# STORMY WEATHER

FERNET MAKES ANOTHER APPEARANCE HERE, THIS TIME MIXED WITH CRÈME DE MENTHE AND DRY VERMOUTH TO MAKE IT SLIGHTLY LESS DISGUSTING. AN ADDED BONUS IS THAT AFTER ONE OF THESE IS YOU'LL HAVE LOVELY MINTY-FRESH BREATH.

★ Add all the ingredients to a shaker filled with ice. Shake and strain into a small highball glass filled with ice and garnish with a sprig of mint.

1 oz. (25 ml) Fernet Branca
1 oz. (25 ml) dry vermouth
2 dashes of crème de menthe
a fresh mint sprig, to garnish

**serves 1**

# BOOZY HOT CHOCOLATE
## with churros

HOT CHOCOLATE SPIKED WITH ORANGE LIQUEUR IS GENIUS, APPEALING TO A DIVERSE CROWD: FRUIT LOVERS, CHOCOLATE LOVERS, COINTREAU LOVERS, AND SWEET-TOOTHED ALCOHOLICS. MAKE CHURROS TO GO WITH IT AND IMAGINE YOU'RE IN SPAIN BEING ALL COSMOPOLITAN, INSTEAD OF CRUSTING ON THE SOFA IN YOUR BOXERS.

### hot chocolate

9 oz. (250 g) bittersweet (dark) chocolate, chopped

2½ cups (600 ml) milk, boiled

4 shots of orange liqueur, such as Cointreau

### churros

5 cups (350 g) self-rising flour

½ teaspoon salt

1 egg, beaten

2 cups (450 ml) milk

light olive oil, for deep-frying

⅓ cup (120 g) superfine (caster) sugar

¼ cup (4 tablespoons) ground cinnamon (optional)

a pastry (piping) bag fitted with a ½–1 in. (1–2 cm) plain nozzle

**serves 4**

★ To make the hot chocolate, mix the chocolate and boiled milk together in a small saucepan, beating and cooking until the chocolate is well blended and the liquid is dusky brown. Pour into 4 cups and add a shot of orange liqueur to each.

★ For the churros, sift the flour and salt in a bowl and make a well in the center. Beat the egg in a bowl with 1 cup (250 ml) of milk. Pour into the well and whisk into the flour. Gradually whisk in enough of the remaining milk to make a smooth, thick batter able to be piped easily. Transfer to the pastry (piping) bag.

★ Pour a 4-in. (10-cm) depth of olive oil into a heavy-based saucepan fitted with a frying basket or electric deep-fat fryer. Heat the oil to 375°F (190°C), or until a cube of bread browns in 35 seconds. It is essential to cook the extruded batter in very hot olive oil in order to crisp and seal the outside and steam the batter inside.

★ Pipe long, spiraled, coiled-up lengths of batter directly into the oil. Leave to sizzle and cook for 4–6 minutes, or until golden and spongy in the center (test one to check).

★ Lift the churros out of the oil using the basket or tongs. Drain on crumpled paper towels. Repeat using the remaining doughnut mixture.

★ When cool, scissor-snip the churros into 6-in. (15-cm) lengths. Put the superfine (caster) sugar in a plate, mix in the cinnamon, if using, then roll the churros in the mixture.

# CHAPTER 6

# HUNGER BUSTERS

## CRUNCHY ROAST PORK
### with baked stuffed apples

**SO YOU'VE DRAGGED YOURSELF OUT OF BED AND YOU'RE STARVING HUNGRY—THIS IS WHAT YOU SHOULD BE COOKING. IT SERVES 6, SO IS PERFECT FOR APOLOGIZING TO HOUSEMATES FOR LAST NIGHT'S DRUNKEN ANTICS. NOTHING SAYS SORRY FOR VOMITING COPIOUSLY ON THE CARPET LIKE A NICE BIT OF ROAST PORK.**

3½-lb. (1.5-kg) loin of pork, boned and rolled

3 eating apples

1 onion, chopped

8 sage leaves, chopped

1 tablespoon olive oil

sea salt and freshly ground black pepper

**gravy**

2 tablespoons all-purpose (plain) flour

1 cup (250 ml) white wine

1 cup (250 ml) vegetable stock

selection of vegetables, to serve

**serves 6**

* Preheat the oven to 425°F (220°C) Gas 7, then lightly oil a roasting pan.

* Dry the loin of pork with paper towels, place in the prepared pan, and roast for 30 minutes. Reduce the heat to 350°F (180°C) Gas 4 and cook the pork for a further 30 minutes.

* Slice the apples in half across the middle and cut out the core. Mix the onion and sage with the oil and season. Arrange the apple halves around the roasting pork and fill the cavities with the stuffing. Return to the oven and cook for 30 minutes. When cooked, transfer the pork and apples to a carving plate and keep warm.

* To make the gravy, drain half the fat from the roasting pan, add the flour, and mix until smooth. Pour in the wine and stock and mix thoroughly. Place the roasting pan directly over the heat and keep stirring until the gravy thickens. Adjust the seasoning. For a very smooth gravy, press it through a sieve. Serve the pork with the roast apples, a selection of vegetables, and the gravy.

# ROAST BEEF WITH ALL THE TRIMMINGS

I WON'T LIE, THERE'S A FAIR BIT OF WORK INVOLVED HERE, BUT NOTHING BEATS A PROPER ROAST DINNER FOR RIGHTING ALL WRONGS AND EASING YOU INTO THAT CONTENTED PLACE WHERE A RESTORATIVE NAP IN FRONT OF THE TV FEELS LIKE THE PERFECT FOLLOW UP. UNLESS YOU'RE A COMPLETE PHILISTINE, DON'T COOK THE BEEF BEYOND MEDIUM-RARE. IF ANYONE COMPLAINS, SHOW THEM THE DOOR AND KICK THEM UNCEREMONIOUSLY OUT ON THEIR ASSES, BANISHING THEM FOREVER. YOU DON'T NEED FRIENDS LIKE THAT.

* Preheat the oven to 475°F (240°C) Gas 8. Season the meat, mix the flour and the mustard and pat it onto the beef fat. Put the dripping or oil in a roasting pan, put the onions in the middle, and set the beef, fat side up, on top. Put the potatoes and parsnips around the meat and put the pan in the preheated oven.

* After 20 minutes cooking time, reduce oven heat to 375°F (190°C) Gas 5, baste the beef and turn the vegetables in the fat.

* To make the Yorkshire pudding batter, put the milk, eggs, flour, and salt in a bowl and whisk well.

* When the roast has been in the oven for 1½ hours, increase the oven temperature to 475°F (240°C) Gas 9 and spoon 4 tablespoons of the fat into a large Yorkshire pudding pan. Heat the fat on the top of the stove and carefully pour the Yorkshire pudding batter into the pan. Put the Yorkshire pudding pan in the oven and cook until well risen, approximately 30 minutes.

* When the beef has been roasting for 1 hour 40 minutes, or when a meat thermometer registers 175°F (60°C) (or a little below if you like beef very rare), take the beef out of the oven. Lift the beef onto a serving dish, add the vegetables, and set aside in a warm place. It will go on cooking as it rests.

* To make the gravy, put the roasting pan on top of the stove, heat the reserved 1 tablespoon fat, add the onion, and cook slowly over low heat until browned, about 30 minutes. Do not let burn. Add the stock and cornstarch (cornflour) mixture, then season to taste with salt and pepper. Stir constantly over low heat until the mixture boils and simmer for a couple of minutes. Strain if you wish or serve as is. Pour into a gravy boat.

* Meanwhile, cook your green vegetables and place in a dish to keep warm. Serve the Yorkshire pudding around the beef or on a separate platter. Put the beef on the table with the gravy and any additional condiments—horseradish sauce is recommended.

6½ lb. (3 kg) bone-in forerib of beef (2–3 bones)

2 tablespoons all-purpose (plain) flour

1 tablespoon hot mustard powder

3 oz. (75 g) beef dripping or shortening, or 4 tablespoons olive oil

3 onions, quartered

8–10 potatoes, cut into chunks and parboiled

5–6 parsnips, halved lengthwise

sea salt and freshly ground black pepper

### Yorkshire pudding

1 cup plus 1 tablespoon (275 ml) milk

2 whole eggs

¾ cup (125 g) all-purpose (plain) flour

½ teaspoon salt

### gravy

1 tablespoon fat from the pan

1 onion, thinly sliced

1 cup (250 ml) beef stock

2 teaspoons cornstarch (cornflour), mixed with 2 teaspoons cold water

sea salt and freshly ground black pepper

3 lb. (1.25 kg) green vegetables, such as cabbage, sliced and steamed or boiled

an instant-read thermometer (optional)

**serves 8–10**

# FISH PIE

FOR PURE FOOD COMFORT FISH PIE IS GUARANTEED TO PUT A SMILE ON ANYONE'S FACE, UNLESS THEY DON'T LIKE FISH... OR MASH. IN WHICH CASE THEY'RE CLEARLY A BIT STRANGE AND SHOULD NEVER BE TRUSTED.

\* Peel the shells from the shrimp (prawns). Put the shells in a saucepan with the milk, onion, bay leaf, and peppercorns. Bring to the boil, then lower the heat and simmer for 10 minutes. Turn off the heat and set aside to infuse.

\* Lay the white and smoked fish fillets, skin side up, in a roasting pan. Strain the infused milk into the pan and and simmer on the stovetop for 5–7 minutes until just opaque. Lift the fish fillets out of the milk and transfer to a plate. When the fillets are cool enough to handle, pull off the skin and flake the fish into large pieces, removing any bones as you go. Transfer to a large bowl and add the shelled shrimp.

\* Melt the butter in a small saucepan set over medium heat, stir in the flour, and gradually add the flavored milk from the roasting pan. Whisk well and simmer gently for 15 minutes until thick and a little reduced. Taste and season with salt and pepper. Stir in the parsley and pour the sauce over the fish. Carefully mix everything together, then transfer the mixture to a pie dish and let cool.

\* Preheat the oven to 350°F (180°C) Gas 4.

\* Boil the potatoes in salted water until soft, drain well, and mash. Beat in the saffron and its soaking water (if using), butter, milk, and dill. When the fish mixture is cold, spoon over the golden mash, piling it up on top. Bake in the preheated oven for 30–40 minutes or until the potato is golden brown and crispy. If it fails to brown enough, finish it off under a medium broiler (grill). Serve immediately.

350 g/12 oz. raw shell-on tiger shrimp (prawns)

3 cups (700 ml) milk

1 onion, chopped

1 bay leaf

2 peppercorns

1 lb. (450 g) fresh sustainable white fish fillets, such as cod, haddock, or pollack, skin on

1 lb. (450 g) undyed smoked haddock or cod fillet, skin on

5 tablespoons (75 g) butter

½ cup plus 1 tablespoon (75 g) all-purpose (plain) flour

4 tablespoons chopped fresh parsley

salt and freshly ground black pepper

**saffron and dill mash**

3 lb. (1.3 kg) floury potatoes, peeled

a large pinch of saffron strands soaked in 3 tablespoons hot water (optional)

5 tablespoons (75 g) butter

1 cup (250 ml) milk

3 tablespoons chopped fresh dill

**serves 4–6**

# BEER CAN CHICKEN

HERE'S A VERSION OF A CLASSIC BBQ RECIPE THAT YOU CAN DO IN THE OVEN, SAVING YOU THE HASSLE OF DRAGGING THE GRILL OUT OF THE GARAGE. FOR THIS RECIPE, THERE ARE FOUR ISSUES TO TAKE INTO CONSIDERATION. THE FIRST IS CHOOSING A BEER. YOU COULD USE A CHEAP CAN, BUT I SUGGEST CHOOSING SOMETHING GOOD AS IT'LL ADD FLAVOR—AN IPA, STOUT, SAISON, OR FRUIT BEER ARE ALL GREAT. THE SECOND ISSUE IS GETTING THE CAN INSIDE THE CHICKEN. THANKFULLY, A BEER CAN IS THE SAME SIZE AS A CHICKEN'S ASSHOLE—IT'S LIKE NATURE INTENDED YOU TO STICK A METAL CYLINDER UP ITS RECTUM! THE THIRD PROBLEM IS MAKING SURE IT DOESN'T FALL OVER. HERE ALL I CAN SUGGEST IS IF YOU SEE IT LEANING OVER, THEN YOU'D BETTER CATCH IT BEFORE IT FALLS (IT WILL!). USEFUL, I KNOW. THE FOURTH PROBLEM IS GETTING THE CAN OUT THE COOKED CHICKEN'S BUTT, BECAUSE THE CHOOK, THE CAN, AND THE BEER STILL LEFT IN THE CAN WILL BE RED HOT. GOOD LUCK WITH THAT!

1 roasting (whole) chicken

1 can of beer

olive oil

a selection of seasoning, herbs, and spices: salt and freshly ground black pepper are essential, the rest are down to you. Try garlic, fresh thyme, and paprika, or you can also go with chili powder, curry powder, or other spices

garlic cloves and fresh thyme (optional)

French fries and coleslaw or salad, to serve

**serves 4–6**

★ Remove all the shelves from the oven apart from the lowest one. Preheat the oven to 400°F (200°C) Gas 6. Place a baking tray in the oven for the chicken to sit on.

★ Now open the can of beer and approach the bird... Rub the oil and your selection of seasoning, herbs, and spices over the bird, plus some of the beer if you wish. If you have some to hand, add some garlic cloves and thyme inside and under the skin of the chicken and to the baking tray for extra flavor.

★ Pour half of the can of beer into a glass. (You can also use this "spare" half can of beer as a brine if you want to start your recipe preparation earlier.) Now, try to push the can inside the chicken—you may need some help with this. Once the can is secure, stand the chicken up and balance it on the baking tray (at this point it may look very sorry for itself, but it'll soon look incredible). Close the oven door and cook for around 1½ hours, depending on the size of the bird.

★ Serve this dish with a plate of fries and some coleslaw or salad. Have a cold beer on the side—it really doesn't matter which one.

# CHICKEN, LEEK, AND TARRAGON POT PIE

PIE! THAT'S JUST WHAT'S NEEDED WHEN YOU'RE FEELING HUNGRY YET FRAGILE AND THE FLAVORS HERE ARE AN ABSOLUTE CLASSIC. USE CHICKEN THIGHS INSTEAD OF BORING BREAST MEAT, AS THEY'RE DIRT CHEAP AND MUCH TASTIER. ALSO, DON'T BE SCARED TO MAKE THE PASTRY, IT'S SUCH A CINCH THAT IT ALMOST FEELS LIKE CHEATING!

1½ cups (185 g) all-purpose (plain) flour

2 tablespoons (30 g) butter

sea salt and freshly ground black pepper

2 tablespoons sour cream

1 egg, lightly beaten

**pie filling**

3 tablespoons (45 g) butter

1½ lb. (750 g) chicken thigh fillets, cut into bite-sized pieces

4 trimmed leeks, sliced

3 tablespoons all-purpose (plain) flour

1 cup (250 ml) chicken stock

½ cup (125 ml) light (single) cream

2 tablespoons chopped fresh tarragon

2 tablespoons roughly chopped fresh flat-leaf parsley,

your choice of vegetables, to serve

**serves 4**

* To make the pastry, process the flour, butter, and a pinch of salt for a few seconds. With the motor running, add the sour cream, half of the beaten egg, and 1–2 tablespoons cold water, until the dough comes together. Roll into a ball, wrap in plastic wrap (clingfilm), and chill for 30 minutes.

* Preheat the oven to 350°F (180°C) Gas 4. Heat half of the butter in a skillet (frying pan) over a high heat. When sizzling, brown the chicken for 2–3 minutes, turning often. Transfer to a bowl. Add the remaining butter to the skillet and cook the leeks over medium heat for 2 minutes. Cover with a lid, reduce the heat, and cook for 2–3 minutes, until really softened.

* Return the chicken to the pan and increase the heat to high. Sprinkle in the flour and cook for 2 minutes, stirring constantly so the flour thickly coats the chicken and leeks. Gradually add the stock, stirring all the time. Bring to the boil, then stir in the cream, tarragon, and parsley. Season well. Reduce heat and simmer until thickened, about 1 minute. Remove from the heat and cool. Spoon into a pie dish.

* Place the dough between 2 pieces of waxed (greaseproof) paper and roll out to a thickness of ¼ in. (5 mm), making sure the dough is more than big enough to cover the dish. Place the dough over the top of the pie, leaving the edges to overhang. Cut several slits in the top of the pie and gently press around the edges with a fork. Brush the remaining beaten egg over the top. Put the pie dish on a baking tray and cook in the preheated oven for 30 minutes, until the pastry is golden.

* Serve with your choice of veg—a heap of buttered new potatoes on the side is recommended.

# STEAK, LEEK, AND MUSHROOM PIE
## with Guinness

**ANOTHER PIE, ANOTHER DELICIOUS FILLING. PIES ARE THE PERFECT COMFORT FOOD FOR FILLING YOU UP AND THERE'S ALMOST NO EFFORT EXPENDED IN MAKING THEM; WINNER-WINNER-PIE-DINNER!**

* Preheat the oven to 325°F (160°C) Gas 3.

* Heat the oil in a large flameproof casserole dish. Add the beef and cook, stirring, for 2–3 minutes, until just browned. Remove the meat from the casserole dish, season, and set aside.

* Add the leeks, onion, and carrots to the dish, adding a little more oil if necessary. Cook over low heat for about 3 minutes, until softened. Add the mushrooms, bacon, and thyme and cook for a further 2–3 minutes. Season well. Add the garlic and cook for 1 minute.

* Return the beef to the dish, add the flour, stir to coat, and cook for 2–3 minutes. Pour in the Guinness and Worcestershire sauce. Add the bay leaf and parsley and pour in cold water to just cover. Stir to mix, cover with a lid, and bake in the oven for 1½ hours.

* Remove the casserole from the oven and increase the oven temperature to 400°F (200°C) Gas 6.

* Transfer the beef mixture to a pie dish. Unroll the pastry and use to cover the pie filling. Fold over the edges and crimp roughly with your fingers. Using a sharp knife, and starting at the top edge, make lengthwise slits on the diagonal, about ⅛ in. (5 mm) apart, all the way across. Brush with melted butter or milk and bake in the preheated oven for about 25–30 minutes, until golden. Serve with mash on the side, made with so much butter you'll feel your arteries harden as you eat it. As a cursory nod to any five-a-day guilt, cook up a big bowl of peas and smother them in butter as well.

1 tablespoon vegetable oil

1½ lb. (700 g) stewing beef, cut into bite-sized pieces

2 trimmed leeks, sliced

1 onion, coarsely chopped

2 large carrots, peeled and diced

9 oz. (250 g) mushrooms, coarsely chopped

3 bacon slices, coarsely chopped

1 teaspoon dried thyme

2 garlic cloves, crushed

2 tablespoons all-purpose (plain) flour

1 12-oz. (330-ml) can Guinness

2 tablespoons Worcestershire sauce

1 bay leaf

a handful of fresh flat-leaf parsley, chopped

13-oz. (375-g) pack ready-rolled puff pastry, defrosted if frozen

melted butter or milk, to brush

sea salt and freshly ground black pepper

buttery mashed potatoes and peas, to serve

**serves 4–6**

# CHILI CON CARNE

I LOVE CHILI AND OFTEN COOK UP A HUGE POT TO EAT OVER A FEW DAYS. IT'S EASY, CHEAP, AND TASTES BETTER THE NEXT DAY ONCE IT'S SETTLED A BIT. IF YOU LIKE IT HOT, ADD A DICED SCOTCH BONNET OR TWO, SEEDS AND ALL, SOME PICKLED JALAPENOS, AND DASHES OF TABASCO AT THE END OF COOKING.

2 tablespoons olive oil

2 onions, diced

3 garlic cloves, crushed

1½ lb. (700 g) lean ground (minced) beef

2 tablespoons tomato paste

2⅓ cups (600 ml) passata (if you can't find use canned chopped tomatoes)

1 tablespoon cayenne pepper

1 tablespoon Spanish smoked sweet paprika

2 14-oz.(400-g) cans red kidney beans, drained

sea salt and freshly ground black pepper

3 tablespoons chopped fresh cilantro (coriander) leaves

white rice and guacamole (optional), to serve

**serves 4–6**

* Heat the oil in a large saucepan or flameproof casserole dish, add the onions and garlic, and fry gently for 5 minutes. Add the beef, breaking it up with a wooden spoon, and cook for a further 5 minutes or until browned. Stir in the tomato paste, passata, cayenne pepper, and paprika and season well.

* Cook on a low heat for 1–1½ hours, stirring occasionally, and reduce until the sauce has thickened. Add the kidney beans and cook for 10 minutes to warm through.

* Just before serving, stir in the chopped cilantro (coriander) and serve with white rice and a bowl of guacamole, if liked.

# BOEUF BOURGUIGNON

YOU'VE JUST DISCOVERD THERE'S A BOTTLE OF RED LEFTOVER (AMAZING!) FROM YESTERDAY'S BOOZING. THEREFORE I MUST INSIST THAT YOU RUSTLE UP A BOUEF BOURGUIGNON—A FRENCH CLASSIC THAT'S HARDLY ANY EFFORT TO MAKE BUT WILL ENSURE YOU'RE STUFFED SILLY WITH LOVELY GALLIC COMFORT GRUB. IF YOU'RE ORGANIZED, THIS (AS WITH ALL CASSEROLES) IS BEST MADE THE DAY BEFORE TO ALLOW THE FLAVORS TO DEVELOP.

* Pat the meat dry, trim off any excess fat or sinew, and cut into large chunks. Heat 1 tablespoon of the oil and fry the pancetta until lightly browned. Remove from the pan with a slotted spoon and transfer to a flameproof casserole dish. Brown the meat in 2 batches in the fat that remains in the pan and add to the pancetta. Add the remaining oil and fry the onion slowly, covering the pan, until soft and caramelized (about 25 minutes), adding the garlic halfway through the cooking time.

* Stir the flour into the onions, cook for a minute, then add the wine and bring to the boil. Pour over the meat, add the bouquet garni, and bring back to the boil. Turn down the heat and simmer over very low heat for 2–2½ hours, until the meat is tender.

* Turn off the heat and leave the casserole overnight, if you wish. The next day bring the casserole back to boiling point, then turn down low again.

* Heat the butter in a skillet (frying pan) and fry the mushrooms until lightly browned (about 5 minutes). Tip the mushrooms into the stew, stir, and cook for another 10–15 minutes. Season the casserole to taste, adding an extra splash of wine if you don't think the flavor is quite pronounced enough. Sprinkle over chopped parsley before serving with mashed potatoes and your choice of greens.

2 lb. (900 g) beef chuck, braising beef, or steak

3 tablespoons olive oil

4½ oz. (130 g) cubed pancetta

3 onions, finely chopped

2 large garlic cloves, finely chopped

1½ tablespoons all-purpose (plain) flour

2 cups (500 ml) full-bodied red wine, plus an extra splash if needed

a bouquet garni made from a few sprigs of thyme, parsley stalks, and a bay leaf

2 tablespoons (30 g) butter

4 oz. (250 g) cremini (chestnut) mushrooms, cleaned and halved

2 tablespoons finely chopped fresh flat-leaf parsley

sea salt and freshly ground black pepper

mashed potatoes and green vegetables, to serve

**serves 6**

# SMOKEY SAUSAGE AND BEAN CASSEROLE

IF YOU CRAVE SOME CAMPFIRE FOOD BUT THE ACT OF ACTUALLY CAMPING SOUNDS LIKE TOO MUCH HARD WORK, TRY THIS RECIPE. WHILE IT'S BUBBLING AWAY, MAKE A "CAMP" IN THE LOUNGE OUT OF PILLOWS AND EAT YOUR FOOD IN THERE, SAFE FROM THE OUTSIDE WORLD. WHO CARES THAT YOU'RE 39 AND A COMPANY DIRECTOR?

1 tablespoon olive oil

12 chipolata sausages

1 garlic clove, chopped

1 leek, thinly sliced

1 carrot, diced

1 celery stick, diced

1 14-oz. (400-g) can chopped tomatoes

1 teaspoon Spanish smoked paprika

2 tablespoons maple syrup

2 sprigs of fresh thyme

1 14-oz. (400-g) can cannellini beans, drained

toasted sourdough bread, to serve

**serves 4**

★ Heat the oil in a heavy-based saucepan over high heat. Add the sausages in 2 batches and cook for 4–5 minutes, turning often until cooked and an even brown all over. Remove from the pan and set aside.

★ Add the garlic, leek, carrot, and celery and cook for 5 minutes, stirring often. Add the tomatoes, paprika, maple syrup, thyme, beans, and 2 cups (500 ml) water and return the sausages to the pan.

★ Bring to the boil, then reduce the heat to medium and simmer for 40–45 minutes, until the sauce has thickened.

★ Put a slice of toasted sourdough on each plate, spoon the casserole on top, serve.

## Variation

Replace the sausages with 1 lb. (450 g) pork neck fillet cut into 1-in. (2.5-cm) pieces. Cook the pork in batches for 4–5 minutes each batch, turning often so each piece is evenly browned. Return all the pork to the pan, as you would the sausages, and simmer for 45–50 minutes until the pork is tender.

# PROVENÇAL-STYLE LAMB CASSEROLE

2¼ lb. (1 kg) lamb leg meat (fat removed), cut into 1-in. (2.5-cm) cubes

2 tablespoons olive oil

1 large onion, chopped

3 carrots, roughly chopped

3 large garlic cloves, crushed

2 large tomatoes, deseeded and chopped

1 tablespoon herbes de Provence

2 cups (500 ml) hot lamb, chicken, or vegetable stock

1 14-oz. (400-g) can butter beans, drained

1 medium–hot red chili, deseeded and cut into strips

1–2 tablespoons cornstarch (cornflour) (optional)

sea salt and freshly ground black pepper

**marinade**

2 sprigs of fresh rosemary

3 fresh bay leaves

6 juniper berries

1 celery stick, chopped

2 strips orange zest

1 bottle dry red wine

boiled new potatoes or fresh garlic bread, to serve

**serves 4**

WE HEAD TO THE SOUTH OF FRANCE FOR THIS ONE, BUT NOT TO CAVORT PLAYBOY-STYLE ON A YACHT IN MONACO OR DRIVE THROUGH THE BEAUTIFUL PROVENÇAL COUNTRYSIDE, SURROUNDED BY LANES BANKED WITH WILD HERBS AND ANCIENT FARMHOUSES. NO, WE'LL BE MAKING THIS (ADMITTEDLY LOVELY) STEW IN YOUR TINY APARTMENT IN THE FREEZING, GRAY CITY WHERE IT'S RAINING OUTSIDE, SEEMINGLY FOR MONTHS. DEAL WITH IT.

* Put all the marinade ingredients in a small, heavy-based saucepan over medium heat and bring to the boil. Reduce the heat and simmer for about 20 minutes until the contents have reduced by about half. Strain the marinade into a large bowl and set aside to cool until nearly room temperature.

* Place the lamb pieces in the marinade, cover, and refrigerate for at least 2 hours.

* Heat the oil in a flameproof casserole dish over medium heat. Remove the lamb from the marinade (reserving the marinade) and add to the hot oil. Fry, stirring constantly, until evenly browned—about 5 minutes. Remove the meat from the dish and set aside.

* Fry the onion in the same pan for about 2 minutes, then add the carrots and garlic. Fry for a further 3 minutes. Add the tomatoes, Provençal herb blend, and reserved marinade and season with salt and pepper. Bring the mixture back to the boil, then add the lamb pieces and stock. Return to the boil, reduce the heat, and add the beans and chili. Simmer for 30–35 minutes, uncovered, or until the lamb is tender.

* About 10 minutes before cooking is complete, take a tablespoon or 2 of the stock from the pan and mix with the cornstarch (cornflour) to form a paste. Stir this paste back into the casserole. This step is optional but will slightly thicken the casserole over the last few minutes of cooking.

* Serve in large bowls with boiled new potatoes or fresh garlic bread.

# CHICKEN TIKKA MASALA

THE NATIONAL DISH OF THE UK! THIS HOMEMADE VERSION IS MUCH NICER THAN THE TAKEAWAY CRAP YOU WERE DRUNKENLY SHOVELING DOWN YOUR NECK THE PREVIOUS EVENING, DIRECT FROM THE FOIL CONTAINER. I SUGGEST YOU ACCOMPANY THE GRUB WITH A HAIR-OF-THE-DOG PINT OF COBRA LAGER AND FOLLOW IT UP BY BRIEFLY MICROWAVING A DAMP CLOTH FROM THE BATHROOM TO GIVE YOUR HANDS A WIPE. AUTHENTIC!

* To make the chicken tikka marinade, combine the yogurt, lemon juice, cumin, cinnamon, cayenne, black pepper, and ginger in a large glass bowl and season with salt. Stir in the chicken, cover, and refrigerate for 4–6 hours or overnight.

* Thread the marinated chicken on to metal skewers (discarding the marinade). Cook under a hot, preheated broiler (grill) for about 5 minutes on each side.

* Meanwhile, make the tikka masala sauce. Melt the butter in a large, heavy skillet (frying pan) over medium heat. Sauté the garlic and chili for 1 minute. Add the cumin and paprika and season well.

* Purée the tinned tomatoes in a blender until smooth, then add to the skillet with the tomato paste and cream. Simmer over low heat until sauce has thickened, about 20 minutes.

* Add the broiled chicken to the pan and simmer for 10 minutes, or until cooked through. Transfer to a serving platter and garnish with the cilantro (coriander) and chili. Serve with warm naan or basmati rice.

---

4 boneless, skinless chicken breasts, cut into bite-sized pieces

salt and freshly ground black pepper

fresh cilantro (coriander) leaves, chopped, to garnish

1 red chili, sliced, to garnish

### chicken tikka marinade

1 cup (250 g) plain yogurt

1 tablespoon freshly squeezed lemon juice

2 teaspoons ground cumin

1 teaspoon ground cinnamon

2 teaspoons cayenne pepper

2 teaspoons freshly ground black pepper

1 tablespoon grated ginger

### tikka masala sauce

1 tablespoon (15 g) butter

1 garlic clove, crushed

1 red chili (deseeded if desired), finely chopped

2 teaspoons ground cumin

3 teaspoons paprika

1 7-oz. (200-g) can chopped tomatoes

2 tablespoons tomato paste

¾ cups (200 ml) heavy (double) cream

naan or basmati rice, to serve

### serves 4

# 🔥 LAMB ROGAN JOSH

PERSONALLY, EATING SPICY FOOD MAKES ME FEEL BETTER WHEN I'M HANGING, BUT RECENTLY I WAS GUTTED TO LEARN THAT SCIENCE HAS DEIGNED THIS ABSOLUTE NONSENSE. STILL, I GUARANTEE YOU'LL FEEL BRIGHTER HAVING EATEN THIS CURRY AND THAT'S ALL THAT MATTERS.

2 tablespoons safflower (sunflower) oil

1¾ lb. (800 g) boneless lamb shoulder, cut into bite-sized pieces

2 large onions, thickly sliced

3 garlic cloves, crushed

2 teaspoons grated ginger

2 cinnamon sticks

2 teaspoons chili powder

2 teaspoons paprika

6 cardamom pods

4 tablespoons medium curry paste

1 14-oz. (400-g) can chopped tomatoes

6 tablespoons tomato paste

1 teaspoon sugar

⅔ cup (150 ml) lamb stock

4–6 potatoes, peeled and left whole

a handful of fresh cilantro (coriander) leaves, chopped

plain yogurt, to serve

**serves 4**

* Heat 1 tablespoon of the oil in a large flameproof casserole dish or heavy-based saucepan. Add the lamb in batches and cook for 3–4 minutes, until evenly browned. Remove with a slotted spoon and set to one side.

* Add the remaining oil to the casserole and add the onions. Cook over medium heat for 10–12 minutes, stirring often, until soft and lightly browned.

* Add the garlic, ginger, cinnamon, chili powder, paprika, and cardamom pods. Stir-fry for 1–2 minutes, then add the curry paste. Stir-fry for 2–3 minutes, then stir in the canned tomatoes, tomato paste, sugar, stock, and potatoes. Season well, bring to a boil, and add the lamb back to the dish.

* Simmer gently for 45 minutes to 1 hour, until the lamb is tender and the sauce has thickened. To serve, add the cilantro (coriander) and drizzle with yogurt.

4 chicken legs (thigh and drumstick)

lemon or lime wedges, to serve

**jerk seasoning paste**

3–4 habanero chilis, deseeded

1 teaspoon fresh thyme, chopped

3 garlic cloves, coarsely chopped

1 bay leaf

1 teaspoon allspice berries (about 20)

¼ teaspoon freshly grated nutmeg

3 scallions (spring onions), chopped

2 plum tomatoes, skinned (fresh or canned)

freshly squeezed juice of ½ lime

5 tablespoons peanut oil

½ teaspoon salt

**serves 4**

# JERK CHICKEN

WHEN A HEAVY NIGHT HITTING THE MALIBU, FOLLOWED BY A HEAVY MORNING REGURGITATING IT, LEAVES YOU FEELING A BIT EMPTY, WHAT YOU NEED TO FILL THAT GAP IS TO STAY WITH THE JAMAICAN THEME AND MAKE YOURSELF SOME JERK CHICKEN. THERE ARE AS MANY JERK RECIPES IN JAMAICA AS THERE ARE COOKS, BUT ALL INCLUDE THE SCOTCH BONNET CHILI OR THE CLOSELY RELATED HABANERO, PLUS A GOOD WHACK OF ALLSPICE.

★ To make the jerk seasoning paste, put all the ingredients in a mortar and pestle and grind to a smooth paste.

★ Cut slashes in the chicken legs and spread with half the jerk seasoning paste. Rub the paste all over and into the slashes, cover, and marinate in the refrigerator for at least 2 hours or overnight.

★ Preheat the oven to 400°F (200°C) Gas 6. Put the chicken legs skin side down into a roasting pan. Roast them in the preheated oven for 40–45 minutes or until crisp and cooked through, turning halfway through the cooking time and coating with the remaining marinade.

★ To cook on a barbecue, preheat a grill until very hot. Cook the chicken over high heat to begin with, then adjust the rack further away from the heat as soon as the surfaces of the chicken have begun to brown. Cook for 15–20 minutes or until done, turning frequently and basting with the remaining marinade. You must cook poultry thoroughly so there is no pink inside: if you have an instant-read thermometer, it should read 165°F (75°C) when inserted into the thickest part of the thigh.

★ Serve hot with lemon or lime wedges on the side for squeezing.

### tomato relish

1 tablespoon olive oil

1 onion, sliced

1 garlic clove, crushed

1 fresh red chili, chopped

2 14-oz. (400 g) cans chopped tomatoes

¾ cup (200 ml) red wine vinegar

1 cup (200 g) sugar

3 tablespoons capers, rinsed

3 or 4 baby gherkins, chopped

a handful of fresh cilantro (coriander)

sea salt and freshly ground black pepper

### burger

12 oz. (340 g) lean ground (minced) beef

a large pinch of sea salt and freshly ground black pepper

1 tablespoon olive or vegetable oil

2 bacon slices

4 Cheddar cheese slices

2 large burger buns

butter, for spreading

2 tablespoons American mustard

2 pickled gherkins, thinly sliced

1 cup (75 g) chopped lettuce

French fries, to serve

**serves 2**

# ULTIMATE RESTAURANT BURGER
## with bacon, cheese, and tomato relish

THIS RECIPE IS SUPERB FOR WHEN YOU FANCY A TOP-NOTCH BURGER, BUT ARE SO HOLLOW EYED AND HANGING THAT THE IDEA OF SETTING FOOT IN A RESTAURANT AND BEING SEEN IN PUBLIC BRINGS YOU OUT IN A COLD SWEAT. ALL THE GOOD STUFF IS HERE—CRACKING BEEF, BACON, CHEESE—AND FEEL FREE TO ADD EXTRA TOPPINGS.

* To make the tomato relish, heat the oil in a skillet (frying pan) set over medium heat. Add the onion, garlic, and chili and fry, stirring occasionally, until soft.

* Add the tomatoes and mix well. Add the vinegar and sugar and bring to the boil. Reduce the heat and simmer for 30 minutes. Season with salt and pepper, to taste. The relish should be the consistency of jam. Stir in the capers, gherkins, and the cilantro (coriander). Taste and adjust the seasoning, if necessary.

* To make the burgers, put the beef in a bowl with the salt and pepper. Work together with your hands until evenly mixed. Divide the beef mixture in half and shape into two burger patties. Press each burger down to make them nice and flat.

* Heat the oil in a skillet (frying pan) and fry the burgers over medium–high heat for 5 minutes on each side until cooked through.

* Meanwhile, heat a separate skillet until hot and fry the bacon slices until crisp. Remove from the pan and set aside.

* When the burgers are cooked, remove from the pan and top each with two slices of cheese. Set aside to allow the cheese to melt slightly.

* Slice the burger buns in half and lightly toast them under the broiler (grill) or in the toaster.

* Spread butter on the cut sides of each bun. Squeeze a little mustard onto the base and put the cooked burgers on top. Add a generous spoonful of tomato relish to each and top with the bacon, gherkins, and lettuce. Finish the burgers with the lids of the buns and serve with fries.

# HONEY-FRIED CHICKEN

HOW GOOD DOES THIS RECIPE SOUND, EH? IT'S GOT A KIND OF HARRY POTTER BUTTERBEER SOUNDING RING TO IT, BUT UNLIKE THE FICTIONAL DRINK LOVED BY THE HOGWARTS CREW, IT'S A REAL THING THAT'S BIG IN THE AMERICAN SOUTH. I SUGGEST YOU MAKE SOME RIGHT AWAY AND STUFF YOURSELF SILLY. BUT PLEASE, IN YOUR HASTE TO GET CHICKEN DOWN YOUR NECK, BE CAREFUL WITH THE DEEP-FAT FRYER AND DON'T BURN ANY BITS OFF. OK?

4 lb. (1.8 kg) whole chicken, cut into pieces

sea salt and freshly ground black pepper

½ cup (170 g) runny honey

1 tablespoon garlic powder

1 packet chicken bouillon granules

2 cups (260 g) all-purpose (plain) flour

4 cups (1 liter) vegetable oil, for frying

Creamed corn or baked beans, to serve (optional)

**serves 4**

★ Season chicken pieces with salt and pepper, then coat each seasoned chicken piece with honey.

★ In a shallow dish or bowl, mix together the garlic powder, chicken bouillon granules, and flour. Dredge the honey-coated chicken pieces in the flour mixture, coating completely.

★ Fill a large, heavy-based skillet (frying-pan) with oil to a depth of 1 in. (2.5 cm) and heat over a medium-high heat until the oil is bubbling steadily.

★ In batches, fry the chicken for at least 8 minutes per side, until it's no longer pink and until the juices run clear. Make sure you heat the oil back up so it's bubbling steadily before frying the next batch. Eat straight away or serve with some creamed corn or baked beans on the side.

# CHAPTER 7

# CARB LOADING

## MASHED POTATO PIE with bacon, leeks, and cheese

ONE OF MY FAVORITE THINGS—MASHED POTATO, IN A PIE. ARE YOU DREAMING? NO! THIS IS ACTUALLY A THING THAT WILL FIX YOUR HANGOVER, LOADING YOU UP WITH ALL THE CARBS YOU COULD EVER NEED. ALTERNATIVELY, A BOWL OF REALLY GOOD BUTTERY MASH SCATTERED WITH FRIED BACON AND LEEKS, THEN COVERED WITH GRATED CHEESE COULD BE A QUICK, SLIGHTLY SLUTTIER ALTERNATIVE. DID I MENTION I LOVE MASH?

2¼ lb. (1 kg) floury potatoes, peeled

2 tablespoons olive oil

1 onion, finely chopped

2 small leeks, thinly sliced

½ cup (80 g) diced thick-sliced bacon or pancetta

2 tablespoons (30 g) butter

1 cup (250 ml) milk or light (single) cream (or a bit of both)

1 egg, beaten

a large handful of fresh parsley leaves, chopped

a pinch of paprika

⅔ cup (90 g) grated firm cheese, such as Gruyère

sea salt and freshly ground black pepper

**serves 4–6**

★ Halve or quarter the potatoes depending on their size; they should be about the same to cook evenly. Put them in a large saucepan, add sufficient cold water to cover, salt well, and bring to a boil. Simmer for about 20 minutes, until tender and easily pierced with a skewer.

★ Meanwhile, heat the oil in a skillet (frying pan) set over a low heat. Add the onion and leeks and cook gently for about 10 minutes, until soft. Add the bacon and cook for 3–5 minutes, until just browned. Season with salt and set aside.

★ Preheat the oven to 375°F (190°C) Gas 5.

★ Drain the potatoes and mash coarsely, mixing in the butter and milk. Season well and add the egg. Stir to combine thoroughly.

★ Stir in the leek mixture, parsley, paprika, and half the cheese. Transfer to a large well-buttered baking dish and spread evenly. Sprinkle over the remaining cheese and bake in the preheated oven for 35–45 minutes, until well browned. Serve immediately.

# SHOOTER'S SANDWICH

THIS WAS A FAVORITE SNACK OF EDWARDIAN GENTS OUT FOR A SPOT OF SHOOTING. MADE THE NIGHT BEFORE A HUNT (OR IN YOUR CASE, A BOOZE UP), PRESSED, AND CUT INTO WEDGES, IT'S PERFECT GRUB FOR WHEN YOU'RE BLOWING AWAY WILD ANIMALS LIKE A BOSS. NOW, I DO REALIZE THAT RATHER THAN STRIDING ACROSS THE MOORS CLAD HEAD TO TOE IN TWEED, SHOTGUN OVER YOUR ARM, YOU'RE MORE LIKELY TO BE SPRAWLED ACROSS THE SOFA, PLAYING CALL OF DUTY IN YOUR PJ'S, BUT WHATEVER, IT'S A LOVELY SANDWICH THAT DOES THE JOB.

## duxelles

2 tablespoons (30 g) butter

8 shallots, very finely chopped

14 oz. (400 g) button mushrooms, finely chopped

a sprig of fresh thyme, leaves picked

2 garlic cloves, crushed

a splash of brandy

sea salt and freshly ground black pepper, to taste

2 steaks, such as rib-eye or sirloin, which will fill the loaf (the size of each steak will depend on the size of loaf used)

1 large round white cob loaf

horseradish sauce

Dijon mustard

**serves 6**

★ First, make the duxelles by melting the butter in a skillet (frying pan) and cooking the shallots and mushrooms slowly until almost all the moisture is gone. Add the thyme, garlic, and brandy and cook again until reduced and nearly all the brandy has cooked off. Season with salt and pepper. Remove from the heat and set aside.

★ Cook the steaks by heating a ridged griddle pan until screaming hot, then season the steaks heavily with salt and pepper just before putting them into the pan. Cook until medium-rare.

★ Cut off the top third of the loaf to make a lid, then hollow out the rest, reserving the crumb for use in another recipe. Spread some horseradish sauce on the bottom of the loaf, then add the first steak, followed by the duxelles. Add the second steak. Don't worry if it pokes out of the top, as the sandwich will be pressed overnight. Spread Dijon mustard on the cut side of the lid, then put the lid back on the loaf.

★ Wrap the sandwich in wax (greaseproof) paper and tie it up with string. Do this tightly. Wrap the whole thing in aluminum foil, then put it in the refrigerator where it can rest overnight. Weigh the top of the sandwich down with something good and heavy. This may require several heavy pans or whatever you have at your disposal. Just make sure it's properly pressed.

★ The next day, remove the weights and remove and discard the wrappings, then cut the loaf into wedges and serve.

# SAUSAGES 'N' MASH with red onion gravy

CLASSIC PUB GRUB AT ITS FINEST, WHO DOESN'T LIKE A PLATE OF MASH, PILED WITH BANGERS AND SMOTHERED WITH ONION GRAVY? I'M A MASH FIEND AND I HAVE A COUPLE OF TIPS TO HELP YOU MAKE SUBLIME MASHED SPUDS. FIRSTLY, BUY A POTATO RICER, YOU'LL NEVER LOOK BACK—NO LUMPS EVER AND THE CREAMIEST, SMOOTHEST MASH GOING. SECONDLY, BEAT LOADS OF BUTTER IN AT THE END WITH A WOODEN SPOON. LASTLY, WHEN SEASONING USE WHITE PEPPER—COPIOUS AMOUNTS. FINALLY, TRY TO USE QUALITY SAUSAGES, NOT CHEAP PINK BANGERS FULL OF MYSTERY MEAT. NO!

★ For the gravy, melt 3 tablespoons (45 g) of the butter in a saucepan and gently fry the onions, garlic, and thyme with a little seasoning for 15–20 minutes, or until soft and lightly golden. Add the port (or red wine), boil rapidly for 1 minute, then add the stock. Simmer for 10 minutes, or until reduced by half. Strain the sauce through a fine strainer and return to the pan. Reserve the onions. Simmer gently over low heat and beat in the remaining butter a little at a time until the sauce is glossy. Return half the onions to the pan, heat, and serve hot.

★ Next, boil the potatoes in a large pan of salted water until soft and tender. This should take 15–20 minutes depending on the size of the potatoes. Drain the potatoes, return them to the pan along with the butter and milk, and mash until smooth. Season with salt and pepper then stir through a tablespoon or two of wholegrain mustard to taste.

★ While the potatoes are cooking, broil (grill) the sausages for 15 minutes until cooked, turning every few minutes.

★ To serve, put a good spoonful of mash onto a plate, add 2 or 3 sausages on top, and cover with onion gravy.

## gravy

5 tablespoons (75 g) unsalted butter, chilled and diced

2 onions, thinly sliced

1 garlic clove, peeled and crushed

1 tablespoon chopped fresh thyme

⅓ cup (80 ml) ruby port (or red wine)

2 cups (500 ml) beef stock

sea salt and freshly ground black pepper

## mash

2 lb. (900 kg) potatoes, peeled and halved

3½ tablespoons (50 g) butter

⅓ cup (80 ml) milk

wholegrain mustard

8 good-quality sausages

**serves 3–4**

# THAI BEEF NOODLE SOUP

I DON'T KNOW WHAT IT IS ABOUT THE HOT, INCREDIBLY CLEAN, AND INTENSE FLAVORS OF THAI FOOD, BUT THERE'S NOT MUCH BETTER WHEN YOU NEED SOOTHING, COMFORTING, AND FILLING FOOD. IF YOU'RE A VEGETARIAN, SKINT, OR BOTH, YOU CAN MAKE THIS RECIPE VEGGIE BY SWITCHING THE BEEF STOCK FOR VEGETABLE STOCK AND LEAVING OUT THE STEAK. TWO PORTOBELLO MUSHROOMS BAKED FOR 20 MINUTES IN A 400°F (200°C) GAS 6 OVEN AND SLICED COULD MAKE A GOOD SUBSTITUTE.

★ To make the broth base, bash the lemongrass carefully with the handle of a knife to bruise it. Place it with all the other broth base ingredients in a saucepan, bring to a simmer, and taste. Add more seasoning if required and discard the lemongrass.

★ For the soup bits and pieces, blanch the noodles in a pan of boiling water for 5 minutes or until cooked, and refresh under cold water.

★ Put the toasted sesame oil in a non-stick skillet (frying pan) and heat. Pour the beaten eggs into the hot pan and fry gently, allowing no color to develop and without stirring. You will eventually get a sort of egg pancake. Let cool slightly to handle, then transfer it to a board and slice it into ⅛-in. (3-mm) strips. Divide the pieces of egg between 2 or 4 soup bowls (depending on how hungry you are).

★ Divide all the remaining ingredients that make up the soup bits and pieces between the bowls, along with the blanched noodles. Bring the broth base back to a simmer, then pour it into the soup bowls—the hot broth will reheat and/or cook all the ingredients. Garnish each bowl with whole cilantro (coriander) leaves, a few slices of chili, a drizzle of sesame oil, and the toasted cashew nuts.

### broth base

1 lemongrass stick

3 cups (750 ml) cold beef stock

2 tablespoons soy sauce

2 tablespoons Thai fish sauce

2 tablespoons palm sugar

grated zest and freshly squeezed juice of 1 lime

1 14-oz. (400-ml) can of coconut milk

### soup bits and pieces

7 oz. (200 g) thin rice noodles, preferably mai fun

2 teaspoons toasted sesame oil, plus extra to drizzle

2 eggs, lightly beaten

2 garlic cloves, crushed

2-in. (5-cm) piece of fresh galangal (or ginger), grated

2 small red chilis, deseeded and thinly sliced, plus extra to garnish

2 kaffir lime leaves

2 big handfuls of spinach leaves

4 chestnut mushrooms, sliced

2 tablespoons chopped fresh cilantro (coriander), plus extra leaves to garnish

2 carrots, cut into matchsticks

4 Baby Gem lettuce leaves, thinly sliced

1 shallot, cut into matchsticks

½ cup (40 g) beansprouts

10 oz. (280 g) sirloin steak, sliced as thinly as you can

4 tablespoons toasted cashews, to garnish

**serves 2–4**

# STIR-FRIED BEEF NOODLES
## with curry paste

THIS STUDENT-STYLE DISH IS EASY ENOUGH, AS LONG AS YOU MUSTER THE ENERGY TO PREP THE VEGETABLES FIRST AND GET EVERYTHING YOU NEED ON THE SIDE READY TO GO. SERIOUSLY, PREPARATION IS THE KEY TO KNOCKING OUT CRACKING STIR-FRIED NOODLES. DON'T BE THAT SAD PERSON MUNCHING ON A BOWL OF NOODLES FULL OF UNIDENTIFIABLE BURNT, GREASY BITS.

4 nests of egg noodles

2 tablespoons peanut or sunflower oil

4 small garlic cloves, finely chopped

1 tablespoon good-quality Thai green curry paste

1 lb (450 g) beef, thinly sliced

1 tablespoon dark soy sauce

3 tablespoons Thai fish sauce

2 teaspoons sugar

1 cup (100 g) beansprouts, rinsed, drained, and trimmed

⅔ cup (100 g) broccoli florets

1 carrot, cut into matchsticks

a handful of fresh cilantro (coriander) leaves, to serve

**serves 4**

★ Cook the noodles according to the package instructions. Drain, rinse, and set aside until needed.

★ Heat the oil in a wok or skillet (frying pan) until hot, add the garlic, and fry until golden brown. Add the Thai green curry paste, stir well, and fry until fragrant.

★ Stirring once after each addition, add the beef, drained noodles, soy sauce, fish sauce, sugar, beansprouts, broccoli, and carrot, and stir-fry over high heat for 2–3 minutes.

★ Mix well and divide the stir-fry between warmed serving bowls and serve immediately, topped with torn cilantro (coriander) leaves.

# CHEESE FONDUE

IT'S KITSCH, CHEESY (LITERALLY), AND MIGHT SEEM LIKE THE MEAL YOU'D GET STUCK INTO WITH OTHER COUPLES BEFORE PUTTING YOUR CAR KEYS IN A BOWL (AND GETTING STUCK INTO SOMETHING ELSE ENTIRELY), BUT IGNORE THE NEGATIVE CONNOTATIONS (AND YOUR MATES WHO THINK YOU'RE A PERVERT); FONDUE IS DAMN TASTY. WHO COULDN'T LOVE BITS AND BOBS STUCK IN HOT CHEESE? I RECKON POTATOES FOR DIPPING AND CORNICHONS ON THE SIDE ARE THE WAY TO GO. OH, AND PARTY PACK OF CONDOMS. JUST KIDDING!

1 garlic clove, halved

1¼ cups (300 ml) dry white wine, such as Sauvignon Blanc

13 oz. (400 g) Gruyère cheese, coarsely grated

13 oz. (400 g) Emmental cheese, coarsely grated

1 tablespoon all-purpose (plain) flour

2–4 tablespoons Kirsch

freshly ground black pepper

2½ lb. (1.25 kg) crusty bread, cut into cubes (about 7 oz./200 g per person), to serve

**serves 6**

* Rub the cut side of the garlic around the inside of the fondue pot. Pour in the wine and bring to a boil on the stove. Reduce the heat to simmering.

* Put the grated cheese into a bowl, add the flour, and toss well. Gradually add the cheese to the wine, stirring constantly, and letting each addition melt into the wine.

* When the mixture is creamy and smooth, add Kirsch and pepper to taste, then transfer the pot to its tabletop burner. Arrange the bread on a platter.

* To eat, spear a piece of bread on a fondue fork, then dip it into the cheese mixture, swirling the fork in a figure-of-eight to keep the fondue smooth.

* To the secrets of successful fondue making include:
- If the fondue is too thick, stir in a little heated wine.
- If it is too thin, add more cheese or stir in a little cornstarch (cornflour) blended with wine.
- If the fondue separates, keep stirring—it should recover. Failing that add a few drops of lemon juice and stir well—or mix 1 teaspoon cornstarch with 2 tablespoons wine, then stir into the cheese.
- Fresh or blanched vegetables make a great alternative to bread.

# MAC 'N' CHEESE

IF YOU REQUIRE CARBS, THIS IS A DELICIOUS WAY TO GET 'EM DOWN YOUR NECK. I'VE KNOCKED OUT A LOT OF MAC 'N' CHEESE IN MY JOB AS A BBQ SMOKESHACK MANAGER AND HAVE A FEW TIPS FOR YOU. FIRSTLY, ONCE YOU'VE RINSED THE JUST-COOKED PASTA IN COLD WATER AND LET IT DRY, TIP INTO A LARGE MIXING BOWL, ADD A TABLESPOON OF VEGETABLE OIL, AND GIVE IT A GOOD MIX. IT'LL STOP THE MACARONI STICKING TOGETHER AND WHEN YOU ADD THE BÉCHAMEL, THE WHOLE LOT WILL SLIDE OUT INTO THE BAKING DISH EASILY—NO STICKING. ALSO, I LIKE TO ADD FEW GRATINGS OF NUTMEG, LIBERAL AMOUNTS OF WHITE PEPPER, AND A FEW CLOVES OF CRUSHED GARLIC TO THE PASTA BEFORE ADDING THE BÉCHAMEL, BUT IT'S UP TO YOU, PEOPLE!

★ Bring a large saucepan of water to the boil. Add the coarse sea salt, then let the water return to a rolling boil. Add the macaroni, stir well, and cook according to the package instructions until very tender. Stir periodically to prevent the macaroni from sticking together. When just cooked, drain, rinse well under cold running water, and let drip dry in a colander.

★ Preheat the broiler (grill) to medium.

★ To make the béchamel sauce, melt the butter in a saucepan. Stir in the flour and cook, stirring constantly, for 1 minute. Pour in the milk in a steady stream, whisking constantly, and continue to whisk for 3–5 minutes until the sauce begins to thicken. Season with fine sea salt. Remove from the heat and add the cheeses, mixing well with a spoon to incorporate. Taste and adjust the seasoning.

★ Put the cooked macaroni in a large mixing bowl. Pour over the hot béchamel sauce and mix well. Taste and adjust the seasoning.

★ Transfer the macaroni mixture to a baking dish and spread evenly. Top with a good grinding of black pepper and sprinkle the breadcrumbs evenly over the top. Broil (grill) for 5–10 minutes until until the top is crunchy and golden brown. Serve immediately.

a handful of coarse sea salt

1 lb. (500 g) macaroni

1 cup (50 g) fresh breadcrumbs

fine sea salt and freshly ground black (or white) pepper

**béchamel sauce**

3½ tablespoons (50 g) unsalted butter

6 tablespoons all-purpose (plain) flour

2½ cups (625 ml) milk

1 teaspoon fine sea salt

1¼ cups (150 g) grated Monterey Jack or other mild, semi-hard cheese

1¼ cups (150 g) grated Cheddar cheese

**serves 6–8**

# LASAGNE

A GOOD LASAGNE IS ACE. RICH BEEF RAGU, PASTA, AND OOZING BÉCHAMEL—I WANT IT... I WANT IT NOW! PEOPLE CAN BE SQUEAMISH ABOUT LIVER; DON'T BE. IT ADDS A DELICIOUS RICHNESS TO THE RAGU, TRUST ME.

★ To make the ragu, cut the pancetta into small cubes. Trim the chicken livers, removing any fat or gristle. Cut off any discolored bits, which will be bitter if left on. Coarsely chop the livers.

★ Melt the butter in a saucepan, add the pancetta, and cook for 2–3 minutes until browning. Add the onion, carrot, and celery and brown these too. Stir in the beef and brown until just changing color, but not hardening—break it up with a wooden spoon. Stir in the chicken livers and cook for 2–3 minutes. Add the tomato paste, mix well, and pour in the wine and stock. Season well with nutmeg, salt, and pepper. Bring to the boil, cover, and simmer very gently for as long as you can—2 hours if possible.

★ For the béchamel sauce, melt the butter in a saucepan. When foaming, add the flour and cook over gentle heat for about 5 minutes without letting it brown. Have a whisk ready. Slide off the heat and add all the milk at once, whisking very well. When all the flour and butter have been amalgamated and there are no lumps, return to the heat and slowly bring to the boil, whisking all the time. When it comes to the boil, add salt and simmer gently for 2–3 minutes.

★ Preheat the oven to 350°F (180°C) Gas 4.

★ Spoon one-third of the meat sauce into a deep, buttered baking dish. Cover with 4 sheets of lasagne and spread with one-third of the béchamel. Repeat twice more, finishing with a layer of béchamel covering the whole top. Sprinkle with Parmesan cheese and bake in the preheated oven for about 45 minutes until brown and bubbling. Let stand for 10 minutes to settle and firm up before serving.

## ragu

3 oz. (75 g) pancetta or dry-cure smoked bacon in a piece

4 oz. (100 g) chicken livers

3 tablespoons (50 g) butter

1 onion, finely chopped

1 carrot, chopped

1 celery stick, trimmed and finely chopped

9 oz. (250 g) ground (minced) beef

2 tablespoons tomato paste

⅓ cup (100 ml) dry white wine

¾ cup (200 ml) beef stock or water

freshly grated nutmeg

sea salt and freshly ground black pepper

## béchamel sauce

5 tablespoons (75 g) butter

⅓ cup (55 g) all-purpose (plain) flour

about 2 cups (500 ml) milk

salt, to taste

about 12 sheets fresh lasagne

½ cup (50 g) freshly grated Parmesan cheese

serves 4–6

# PASTA WITH FRESH TOMATO

THIS DISH ALWAYS ASTOUNDS ME—IT'S SO SIMPLE YET TASTES SO INCREDIBLY FRESH. USE REALLY GOOD VINE TOMATOES—RIPE, DEEP-RED ONES THAT ACTUALLY SMELL AND TASTE LIKE TOMATOES—NOT THE HORRIBLE UNRIPE ONES BELOVED OF MOST SUPERMARKETS. IF PEELING TOMATOES SOUNDS LIKE A MISSION, CHOP THEM INTO ½-IN. (1-CM) PIECES INSTEAD.

2 lb. (900 g) ripe tomatoes

⅓ cup (80 ml) extra virgin olive oil

2 red chilis, deseeded and chopped

2 garlic cloves, crushed

1 tablespoon chopped fresh basil

1 teaspoon sugar

12 oz. (350 g) dried spaghetti

sea salt and freshly ground black pepper

Parmesan cheese, grated, to serve

**serves 4**

★ Holding each tomato with tongs or a skewer, char them over a gas flame until the skins blister and start to shrivel. Peel off the skins, chop the flesh, and put into a bowl. Add the oil, chilis, garlic, basil, sugar, salt, and pepper and leave to infuse while you cook the pasta (or longer if possible).

★ Bring a large saucepan of salted water to a boil. Add the pasta and cook until al dente, or according to the instructions on the package. Drain well and immediately stir in the fresh tomato sauce. Serve at once with the grated Parmesan.

# PENNE WITH SPICY MEATBALLS

**THIS IS AN ABSOLUTE PIECE OF CAKE TO KNOCK OUT. I HAVE NO IDEA HOW AUTHENTICALLY ITALIAN THE RECIPE IS (I SUSPECT NOT VERY!), BUT WHO CARES? YOU'RE HUNGOVER AND IT TASTES GOOD!**

2 tablespoons olive oil

1 onion, chopped

2 garlic cloves, crushed

2 14-oz. (400-g) cans chopped tomatoes

1 tablespoon tomato paste

½ teaspoon superfine (caster) sugar

½ teaspoon dried hot pepper (chili) flakes

14 oz. (400 g) good-quality sausages

4 cups (400 g) dried penne, or other pasta shapes

sea salt and freshly ground black pepper

Parmesan cheese, finely grated, to serve

**serves 4**

★ Heat the oil in a skillet (frying pan) over medium heat. Add the onion and garlic and cook for 2–3 minutes, until soft and just starting to brown. Add the tomatoes, tomato paste, sugar, hot pepper (chili) flakes, and ½ cup (125 ml) water and bring to the boil. Reduce the heat to a simmer.

★ Using slightly wet hands, squeeze the filling out of the sausage casings, and shape into walnut-sized balls. Add these to the tomato sauce. Simmer the meatballs in the sauce for 5 minutes, shaking the pan often to move the meatballs around so that they cook evenly.

★ Bring a large saucepan of water to the boil, add plenty of salt, and return to the boil. Cook the pasta according to the package instructions. Drain the pasta well and return it to the warm pan.

★ Season the meatball sauce with salt and pepper. Divide the pasta between warmed serving plates and top with meatballs. Serve immediately topped with finely grated Parmesan.

# CHAPTER 8

# SUGAR BOMBS

## NUTELLA AND BANANAS ON BRIOCHE (OR TOAST)

4 thick slices brioche bread (or regular bread)

4 tablespoons Nutella (or other chocolate-hazelnut spread)

1 small banana, thinly sliced

vegetable oil, for brushing

**serves 2**

A MASSIVE SCOOP OF NUTELLA NESTLED UP NEXT TO SOME BANANA AND WARMED BETWEEN TWO PIECES OF BUTTERY BRIOCHE. HOLY MOLY, HOW GOOD DOES THAT SOUND? OK, IF YOU'RE A BIT SKINT, OR JUST HAVE ZERO CLASS AND DON'T HAVE BRIOCHE, THEN I'M GOING TO SUGGEST YOU USE TOAST INSTEAD, BUT IT WON'T BE AS NICE.

★ Preheat a sandwich press.

★ Spread 2 slices of the brioche with the Nutella. Place the banana slices on top. Close the sandwiches with the second slice of brioche. Brush both sides of the panini with a little oil and toast in the preheated sandwich press for 2 minutes, or according to the manufacturer's instructions. The bread should be golden brown and the filling warmed through.

### Variation

As an alternative, try replacing the Nutella with a good-quality peanut butter.

# LEMON MERINGUE PIE

THIS PIE IS A THING OF BEAUTY, BUT IT IS A FAIR BIT OF WORK WHEN HUNGOVER. WHAT I SUGGEST IS YOU FLAG THIS PAGE AND DRAG YOURSELF OUT OF BED CLUTCHING THE BOOK, WHIMPERING AS YOU COMPOSE YOUR BEST PLEADING FACE. NEXT, WORDLESSLY POINT AT THE RECIPE AND APPEAL TO THE MERCY OF YOUR PARTNER/HOUSEMATE. YOU NEED LEMON MERINGUE PIE TO RECOVER. YOU'D DO THE SAME FOR THEM, RIGHT?

★ To make the filling, combine 1½ cups (350 ml) cold water, sugar, cornstarch (cornflour), and salt in a saucepan. Over medium/high heat, bring the mixture to the boil, whisking constantly. Remove from the heat.

★ In a medium bowl, whisk the egg yolks. Pour about ½ cup (100 ml) of the sugar mixture into the egg yolks and whisk well. Pour the yolk mixture back into the saucepan. Bring the mixture to the boil over medium/high heat, whisking constantly. Boil for 1 minute then remove from the heat. Whisk in the lemon juice, zest, butter, and finally the vanilla extract. Set aside while you make the meringue topping.

★ Preheat the broiler (grill) and make the meringue. Heat the cornstarch and ⅓ cup (75 ml) water in a small saucepan. Bring to the boil over medium/high heat, stirring constantly. Boil for 30 seconds and remove from the heat.

★ In a large bowl, beat the egg whites with an electric whisk on a low speed until they are frothy. Add the salt and cream of tartar, turn the speed up to medium/high, and beat until the whites form soft peaks. Add the sugar 1 spoonful at a time until the meringue is very glossy. Add a little of the meringue to the cornstarch mixture and stir. Pour this slowly back into the meringue and whisk on high speed until stiff peaks form.

★ Reheat the lemon mixture until hot. Pour this into the pie case. Gently spoon the meringue over the surface, making sure that it adheres to the crust and is well sealed. Use the back of a spoon to make decorative peaks and swirls on top. Put on a rack 6 in. (15 cm) under a very hot broiler for about 5 minutes, or until browned. Leave to cool completely on a rack, then refrigerate until ready to serve. Eat on the same day of preparation.

## filling

scant 1 cup (200 g) granulated (caster) sugar

¼ cup (30 g) cornstarch (cornflour)

a pinch of salt

5 egg yolks

½ cup (125 ml) freshly squeezed lemon juice

1 tablespoon grated lemon zest

3 tablespoons (45 g) unsalted butter

1 teaspoon vanilla extract

## meringue

1 tablespoon cornstarch (cornflour)

5 egg whites

a pinch of salt

¼ teaspoon cream of tartar

½ cup (100 g) superfine (caster) sugar

1 store-bought pie/pastry case

**serves 8**

# BLACKBERRY CRUMBLE

WHAT COULD BE MORE SOOTHING TO YOUR DRINK-RAVAGED NOGGIN THAN AN AUTUMNAL RAMBLE, FORAGING BLACKBERRIES AND NO DOUBT GETTING ENTANGLED, CURSING AND SCREAMING, IN THE BRAMBLES. IF AGAINST THE ODDS YOU DO MANAGE TO COLLECT SOME BERRIES THEN MAKE THIS CRUMBLE, AND SLATHER WITH CREAM OR CUSTARD. PROPER JOB.

3 cups (350 g) blackberries (about 2 punnets)

1 tablespoon granulated (caster) sugar

1 teaspoon cornstarch (cornflour)

1 cup (130 g) plain (all-purpose) flour

5 tablespoons (75 g) unsalted butter, chilled and cubed

¼ cup (60 g) soft light brown sugar

cream or custard, to serve

**serves 4**

★ Put the blackberries in a bowl with the granulated (caster) sugar and the cornstarch (cornflour) and toss to mix. Put the berries in a well-buttered prepared baking dish and set aside for 15–20 minutes.

★ Preheat the oven to 350°F (180°C) Gas 4.

★ Put the flour and butter in a large bowl and, using the tips of your fingers, rub the butter into the flour until the mixture resembles coarse breadcrumbs. Stir in the brown sugar.

★ Sprinkle the mixture evenly over the berries and bake in the preheated oven for 45–50 minutes until the top is golden brown.

★ Leave the crumble to cool slightly before serving with dollops of cream or custard spooned on top.

# CLASSIC HASH BROWNIES

WHEN YOU'RE FEELING ALL DELICATE AND HUNGOVER, I'M NOT SURE THAT THIS CANNABIS CUISINE CLASSIC WILL ACTUALLY MAKE YOU FEEL ANY BETTER, BUT WHATEVER FLOATS YOUR BOAT—THEY SOUND DELICIOUS. MAKE SURE YOU KEEP 'EM AWAY FROM THE MITTS OF INNOCENT, STARVING, AND HUNGOVER FRIENDS, OR THEY MIGHT BE IN FOR A BIT OF A SHOCK!

**cannabutter**

1 stick (110 g) butter

¼ oz (8 g) cannabis, chopped or ground

**brownie**

½ cup (55 g) self-rising flour

½ teaspoon baking powder

⅓ cup (40 g) cocoa powder

¼ cup (25 g) ground almonds

1 cup (225 g) soft brown sugar

zest of 1 large orange, grated

8 tablespoons (120 g) cannabutter

2 eggs

**chocolate frosting**

1 stick (110 g) regular butter or margarine

½–1 cup (25–55 g) cocoa powder

2–2¼ cups (225–275 g) confectioner's (icing) sugar

**makes 16 pieces**

★ For the cannabutter, bring 2½ cups (600 ml) water to boil in a pan. Add the butter and melt.

★ Add the cannabis to the pan, adjusting the amount depending on the strength of your weed. Stir and simmer for 30 minutes, making sure the pan doesn't boil dry. Only a small amount of water should have evaporated from the pan.

★ Strain the liquid into a pint glass and put in the fridge until two layers form. The top (solid) layer is your butter, discard the bottom layer.

★ To make the brownies, sift the flour, baking powder, and cocoa powder into a mixing bowl. Add the ground almonds, sugar, and orange zest and thoroughly mix together.

★ Add the cannabutter and eggs, and then beat the mixture together until smooth.

★ Bake at 300°F (150°C) Gas 2 in a shallow dish, greased with butter and lined with waxed (greaseproof) paper, for about 50 minutes. Leave to cool while you make the chocolate frosting.

★ For the frosting, mix together the ingredients in a bowl and spread it on top of the brownies. Cut the brownies into 16 pieces and serve.

# STICKY TOFFEE PUDDINGS

LOOK, I DON'T CARE THAT YOU SEE IT ALL OVER THE PLACE, I LOVE STICKY TOFFEE PUD! I CAN'T STRESS ENOUGH HOW UNAPOLOGETIC I AM ABOUT THIS, IT'S AN ABSOLUTE FAVORITE. THIS RECIPE IS A GOOD, SIMPLE INTRO TO THIS KING OF DESSERTS, WHICH EXACTLY AS IT SHOULD BE FOR A BOOK ON HANGOVERS. IT SUGGESTS SERVING WITH CREAM OR ICE-CREAM, BUT HOW ABOUT A GALLON OF CUSTARD INSTEAD? I KNOW WHICH GETS MY VOTE.

★ Pour or spoon the dulce de leche into the bottom of 6 individual buttered pudding molds or a buttered pudding basin.

★ Beat together the butter and sugar until pale and creamy, then beat in the eggs, one at a time. Sift over the flour and fold in, then stir in the walnuts. Pour the mixture into the molds or basin.

★ Cover each pudding with 2 sheets of foil and tie firmly in place with a piece of kitchen string.

★ Put the puddings in a large pan and pour boiling water into the pan about two-thirds of the way up the sides of the puddings. Cover with a lid and simmer gently for about 1½ hours, checking the water level occasionally and topping up if necessary.

★ To serve, remove the foil, invert the pudding(s) onto serving plate(s), and lift off. Serve warm with heavy (double) cream or ice cream.

⅓ cup (80 ml) dulce de leche

1 stick (110 g) unsalted butter, at room temperature

⅔ cup (115 g) sugar

2 eggs

¾ cup (115 g) self-rising flour

¼ cup (40 g) walnut pieces

heavy (double) cream or vanilla ice cream, to serve

**serves 6**

# ROCKY ROADIES

THIS IS EXACTLY WHAT YOU NEED WHEN YOU'RE IN AN ABSOLUTE STATE FROM OVER INDULGING ON THE SAUCE—A RICH CHOCOLATE BROWNIE TOPPED WITH PRETTY MUCH ALL THE SUGARY CRAP YOU CAN IMAGINE. THE BEST THING HERE IS PORTABILITY. PEEK YOUR HEAD OUT FROM UNDER THE DUVET AND TAKE A MOMENT FOR YOUR EYES TO ADJUST TO THE AFTERNOON DAYLIGHT STREAMING THROUGH THE WINDOWS. TENTATIVELY TAKE A WOBBLY STEP OUT OF YOUR PIT AND STUMBLE YOUR WAY TO THE KITCHEN. GRAB A PREVIOUSLY MADE SLICE OF BROWNIE AND PINBALL YOUR WAY BACK TO BED. CLAMBER UNDER THE COVERS AND EAT IT THERE, FEELING LIKE A WINNER.

★ Preheat the oven to 325°F (170°C) Gas 3.

★ To make the brownies, put the chocolate and butter in a heatproof bowl set over a saucepan of barely simmering water. Stir until smooth and thoroughly combined. Leave to cool slightly.

★ Add both the sugars and mix well. Add the eggs one at a time, beating well after each addition. Stir in the vanilla extract. Sift the flour and salt into the bowl and stir until smooth.

★ Pour the mixture into a 8 x 12-in. (20 x 30-cm) buttered baking pan, greased and lined with greased baking parchment. Spread the mixture level and bake on the middle shelf of the preheated oven for 20 minutes.

★ Remove from the oven and, working quickly, scatter the marshmallows, nuts, cherries, chocolate chips, and sugar sprinkles evenly over the top.

★ Return the brownies to the oven for a further 3 minutes, or until the marshmallows and chocolate chips are just starting to melt. Remove from the oven and leave to cool completely in the pan before cutting into portions to serve.

8 oz. (225 g) bittersweet (dark) chocolate, chopped

1⅓ sticks (150 g) butter, diced

½ cup plus 1 tablespoon (125 g) superfine (caster) sugar

½ cup plus 1 tablespoon (125 g) light brown (light muscovado) sugar

4 eggs, lightly beaten

1 teaspoon vanilla extract

1 cup (125 g) all-purpose (plain) flour

a pinch of salt

1½ cups (75 g) mini-marshmallows

⅔ cup (75 g) chopped walnuts or pecans

3½ oz. (100 g) glacé cherries, chopped

3½ oz. (100 g) bittersweet (dark) chocolate chips

sugar sprinkles

**makes 16–20**

# TARTE TATIN

IF THE IDEA OF WARM, STICKY, CARAMELIZED APPLES SAT ON CRISP PUFF PASTRY DOESN'T DO IT FOR YOU, THEN CHECK YOUR PULSE TO SEE THAT YOU'RE STILL ALIVE! BE SURE TO PACK THE APPLES IN TIGHT AND FILL IN ALL THE GAPS. IF YOU FANCY GOING A BIT OFF PISTE, SCATTER SOME FINELY CHOPPED ROSEMARY OVER THE APPLES FOR A NICE CHANGE.

1 lb. (450 g) ready-made puff pastry, thawed if frozen

1¼ cups (300 g) sugar

1½ sticks (150 g) chilled unsalted butter, thinly sliced

5 lb.(2½ kg) evenly-sized eating apples such as Golden Delicious, Granny Smith, Braeburn, Cox's, or Jonagolds

crème fraîche or whipped cream, to serve

**serves 6**

★ Roll out the pastry on baking parchment to a circle about 12 in. (30 cm) in diameter. Slide onto a baking sheet and chill. Sprinkle the sugar over the base of an ovenproof tarte tatin dish or cast-iron skillet (frying pan), around 11 in. (28 cm) in diameter. Cover with the slices of butter.

★ Peel, halve, and core the apples. Add the apple halves to the outside edge of the dish—set the first one at an angle, almost on its edge, then arrange the others all around the edge so that they slightly overlap and butt up against each other. Add another ring of apple slices inside, so that the dish is almost filled, then put a whole half to fill the gap in the center.

★ Set the dish over gentle heat and cook for about 45 minutes until the sugar and butter have caramelized and the apples have softened underneath. The juices will gradually bubble up the sides; keep cooking until they are dark amber.

★ Preheat the oven to 325°F (170°C) Gas 3½.

★ Lay the pastry over the apples in the dish and tuck in the edges. Prick the top of the pastry with a fork, then set the dish on the baking sheet. Bake in the preheated oven for 25–30 minutes until the pastry is risen and golden. Remove and invert the tart onto a warm serving plate. Serve warm with crème fraîche or cream.

# TIRAMISÙ

NOW WE'RE TALKING! IF YOUR IDEA OF AN APRÈS BOOZE DESSERT IS ONE SOAKED FULL OF A LOAD MORE ALCOHOL, THEN THIS ITALIAN CLASSIC IS JUST THE TICKET. IF THAT'S NOT SOLD IT TO YOU, I SHOULD ALSO MENTION THE RECIPE IS PRETTY MUCH FOOLPROOF. HELL YES!

25 amaretti cookies (biscuits), crushed

½ cup (100 ml) Kahlúa or other coffee-flavored liqueur

3 tablespoons brandy

4 tablespoons strong black coffee

1 lb. (450 g) mascarpone cheese, at room temperature

6 eggs, separated

¼ cup (50 g) superfine (caster) sugar

4 oz. (125 g) bittersweet (dark) chocolate, grated, or 2 tablespoons unsweetened cocoa

**serves 10**

★ Arrange a quarter of the crushed amaretti cookies at the bottom of 10 glasses or one serving dish. Put the Kahlúa in a small bowl with the brandy and coffee and mix to combine. Pour a quarter of the mixture over the crushed cookies.

★ Put the mascarpone, egg yolks, and superfine (caster) sugar in a bowl and beat until smooth and lump-free. Put the egg whites in a separate, grease-free bowl and whisk until stiff and peaking. Gently fold the egg whites into the mascarpone mixture.

★ Spoon a quarter of the mixture over the cookies, then repeat the layers 3 times, finishing with a layer of mascarpone mixture.

★ Sprinkle the grated chocolate or cocoa over the top of the tiramisù and chill overnight. Serve chilled or at room temperature.

# PEACH COBBLER

UK READERS MAY HAVE A BEMUSED EXPRESSION, THINKING "COBBLERS? IN MY PUDDING? WHAT THE HELL IS GOING ON?" BUT REST EASY BRITS, THERE ARE DEFINITELY NO BALLS INVOLVED IN THIS DISH. A COBBLER IS A FRUIT PUDDING, USUALLY TOPPED WITH BATTER. ON THE OTHER HAND, IF YOU'RE A MAN AND FEEL A LITTLE CHEATED OR DISAPPOINTED, FEEL FREE TO STICK YOUR NUTS IN THE COBBLER, *AMERICAN PIE*-STYLE, JUST LET IT COOL DOWN FIRST.

★ Preheat the oven to 375°F (190°C) Gas 5.

★ Cut the peaches in half, remove the pits (stones), then cut each half into 3 slices. Put them in a shallow ovenproof baking dish, sprinkle with the flour, and toss well to coat evenly. Add the lemon juice and honey and stir. Set aside.

★ For the topping, put the cream and sour cream in a bowl and stir well. Set aside.

★ Put the flour, sugar, baking powder, baking (bicarbonate of) soda, and salt in a large bowl and mix well. Add the butter and mix with your fingertips until the mixture resembles coarse breadcrumbs. Using a fork, stir in the cream mixture until blended. Use your hands at the end if necessary—it should be sticky, thick, and not willing to blend easily.

★ Drop spoonfuls of the mixture on top of the peaches, leaving gaps to expose the fruit. Sprinkle sugar liberally on top of the batter. Bake in the preheated oven for about 25–35 minutes, until golden. Serve warm with cream or ice cream.

6 peaches, not too ripe

1 tablespoon all-purpose (plain) flour

1 tablespoon freshly squeezed lemon juice

3 tablespoons clear honey

pouring cream or vanilla ice cream, to serve

## cobbler topping

½ cup (125 ml) heavy (double) cream

5 tablespoons sour cream or crème fraîche

1¼ cups (165 g) all-purpose (plain) flour

¼ cup (50 g) sugar, plus extra for sprinkling

1 teaspoon baking powder

¼ teaspoon baking (bicarbonate of) soda

a pinch of salt

4 tablespoons (60 g) unsalted butter

**serves 6**

# CARROT AND COCONUT CAKE

ACCORDING TO THE EXHAUSTIVE TWO MINUTES I SPENT RESEARCHING ONLINE, CARROTS ARE ONE OF THE BEST HANGOVER FOODS. CAKE IS ALSO A TOTAL CHAMPION IN THE FEEL-GOOD STAKES. SO WHAT HAPPENS WHEN YOU COMBINE THE TWO? AN ABSOLUTE BEHEMOTH OF A GOOD THING, THAT'S WHAT!

★ Preheat the oven to 350°F (180°C) Gas 4.

★ Put the pecans on a baking sheet and toast in the preheated oven for 7 minutes. Let cool slightly, then roughly chop. Leave the oven on.

★ Sift the flour, baking powder, baking (bicarbonate of) soda, and cinnamon together into a bowl and set aside.

★ In another bowl, whisk together the eggs, sunflower oil, sugar, milk, and vanilla extract and mix until smooth. Add the carrots, orange zest, desiccated coconut, and pecans and mix well. Add the dry ingredients and fold in using a large spoon or spatula until thoroughly combined.

★ Grease and line with greased baking parchment two 8-in. (20-cm) round cake pans. Divide the mixture between the two pans and bake on the middle shelf of the preheated oven for about 40 minutes, or until a skewer inserted into the middle of the cakes comes out clean. Let the cakes cool in the pans for 10 minutes before turning out onto wire cooling racks. Turn the cakes right-side up and let cool completely.

★ To make the frosting, beat the cream cheese and honey together until smooth. Place one of the cake layers on a large plate and spread half the frosting over it. Cover with the second layer and the remaining frosting.

½ cup (75 g) shelled pecans

2¾ cups (375 g) all-purpose (plain) flour

2 teaspoons baking powder

1 teaspoon baking (bicarbonate of) soda

½ teaspoon ground cinnamon

3 large eggs

1½ cups (375 ml) sunflower oil

2¼ cups (450 g) unrefined superfine (caster) sugar

¼ cup (60 ml) milk

1 teaspoon vanilla extract

1 lb. (450 g) carrots, grated

grated zest of 1 orange

1 cup (125 g) desiccated coconut

**frosting**

1 lb. (450 g) cream cheese

2–3 heaped tablespoons clear honey

**serves 8–10**

# THE GREATEST COOKIES

THINK ABOUT THIS... WHEN YOU'VE HAD SO MUCH FUN BOOZING IT UP THE PREVIOUS NIGHT AND WAKE THE NEXT DAY, BARELY ABLE TO FUNCTION, WHAT DO YOU NEED? THAT'S RIGHT, YOU NEED SOMEONE TO LOOK AFTER YOU, TO BRING YOU CUPS OF TEA AND TOAST IN BED, AND PERHAPS SOME PARACETAMOL. MAYBE IT'D BE NICE IF SOMEONE COULD HOLD YOUR HAIR BACK WHILE YOU'RE SWEATING, SHUDDERING, AND PUKING YOUR GUTS UP. NOW, HOW BEST TO RECRUIT AND INCENTIVIZE THIS HELPER, CONSIDERING THAT LOOKING AFTER YOUR HUNGOVER ASS IS NOT EXACTLY A DESIRABLE JOB? THE NIGHT BEFORE, MAKE THESE COOKIES. THEY ARE LOVELY; THEY ARE YOUR INCENTIVE—OFFER THEM IN RETURN FOR THEIR CARE. AND THAT'S WHY THEY ARE "THE GREATEST COOKIES."

7 tablespoons (100 g) butter, at room temperature and chopped

7 tablespoons (80 g) superfine (caster) sugar

3 tablespoons (35 g) muscovado or soft brown sugar

1 teaspoon pure vanilla extract

1 teaspoon light (single) cream

1 egg

scant 1¼ cups (160 g) all-purpose (plain) flour

¼ teaspoon baking powder

¼ teaspoon salt

¾ cup (135 g) bittersweet (dark) chocolate chips

⅓ cup (55 g) walnuts, chopped

**makes about 25**

★ Put the butter in a bowl and beat with a wooden spoon until very soft. Beat in the sugars until well incorporated and creamy, then add the vanilla extract, cream, and egg and beat in. Gradually sift in the flour, baking powder, and salt and mix until combined. Finally, mix in the chocolate chips and walnuts.

★ Cover and refrigerate for 30 minutes.

★ Preheat the oven to 325°F (170°C) Gas 3. Line one or two baking sheets with parchment paper.

★ Remove the bowl from the fridge. Lightly flour a clean work surface and roll the chilled dough out into a sausage roughly 12 in. (30 cm) long. Cut the dough into about 25 equal slices and arrange on the prepared baking sheets.

★ Bake in the preheated oven for about 15–20 minutes until golden brown. Allow the cookies to cool on the baking sheets for 5 minutes, then transfer to a wire rack to finish cooling.

# INDEX

# RECIPE CREDITS

**Miranda Ballard**
Ultimate Restaurant Burger 105

**Fiona Beckett**
Tuna Melt 45
Bouef Bourguignon 96

**Mickael Benichou**
The Greatest Cookies 141

**Vatcharin Bhumichitr**
Stir-fried Beef Noodles 116

**Susannah Blake**
Eggs Florentine 31
Sticky Toffee Puddings 133

**Dominic Bliss**
The Full English 36
Cabbage Soup 61
Fernet 82

**Celia Brooks Brown**
Rarebit 27

**Michael Butt**
Boilermaker 74
Pickleback 74

**Maxine Clark**
Spicy Red Pepper and Tomato
   Soup 67
Fish Pie 88
Lasagne 120
Tarte Tatin 136

**Linda Collister**
French Toast 25
Breakfast Kebabs 26

**Ross Dobson**
Chicken, Leek, and Tarragon Pot
   Pie 92
Steak, Leek, and Mushroom
   Pie 94
Smokey Sausage and Bean
   Casserole 97
Penne with Spicy Meatballs 124
Blackberry Crumble 130

**Dog 'n' Bone Books**
Cereal 18
Pimp My Beans on Toast 43
Last Night's Leftovers 43
Avocado on Toast 44
Fish Stick Sandwich 48
Sausage 'n' Mash 113

**Dr Hash**
Classic Hash Brownies 131

**Mark Dredge**
Beer Can Chicken 91

**Hattie Ellis**
Coffee 18

**Clare Ferguson**
Boozy Hot Chocolate 83

**Manisha Gambhir Harkins**
Jerk Chicken 102

**Tonia George**
Bircher Muesli 56
Porridge with Apples and
   Blackberries 57
Couscous Salad 69

**Victoria Glass**
Cookies and Irish Cream 77
The Elvis 78

**Nicola Graimes**
Green Day 8
Rocket Fuel 9

**Helen Graves**
The Hot Brown 29
Baked Bean Toastie 42
A Good Bacon Sandwich 46
Lox and Cream Cheese Bagel 47
Chip Butty 52
Shooter's Sandwich 110

**Kate Habershon**
Triple Chocolate Pancakes 21
Morning-after Breakfast
   Waffles 22
Belgian Waffles 23

**Carol Hilker**
Honey-fried Chicken 106

**Jennifer Joyce**
Huevos Rancheros 32
Corned Hash Beef 37
Nutella and Bananas on
   Brioche 126
Lemon Meringue Pie 129

**Caroline Marson**
Quick Thai Chicken Curry 55
Roasted Vegetable Soup 66

**Dan May**
Fruity Quinoa and Bean Stew 58
Provençal-style Lamb
   Casserole 99
Thai Beef Noodle Soup 114

**Hannah Miles**
Chocolate Malt Shake 14
Peanut Butter Shake 16
Coffee Frappé 17

**Elsa Petersen-Schepelern**
Frozen Fruit Juice Granitas 10
Mango and Ginger Lassi 11
Banana Breakfast Smoothie 12
Tropical Fruit Smoothie 13
Red Salad 60

**Louise Pickford**
Morning Cleanser 9
Blueberry Muesli Smoothie 11
Frozen Berry Smoothie 12
Hash Browns 24
Eggs Benedict 30
Eggs Cocotte 35
Steak Sandwich 51
Bloody Mary 72
Mulled Mary 72
Mimosa 75
Gravy 113
Pasta with Fresh Tomato 123

**Ben Reed**
Corpse Reviver 71
Vodka Espresso 71
Hot Toddy 80
Prairie Oyster 81
Stormy Weather 82

**Annie Rigg**
Buttermilk Pancakes 19
Blueberry Pancakes 20
Rocky Roadies 134
Carrot and Coconut Cake 139

**Jenny Shapter**
Ultimate Omelet 34

**Fiona Smith**
Caesar Salad 59
Tomato, Avocado, and Lime
   Salad 63
New Potato, Crisp Salami, and
   Sesame Salad 64
Cheese Fondue 117
Mac 'n' Cheese 119

**Sonia Stevenson**
Roast Beef with all the
   Trimmings 86

**Fran Warde**
Crunchy Roast Pork 84
Chili Con Carne 95
Tiramisù 137

**Sunil Vijayakar**
Chicken Tikka Masala 100
Lamb Rogan Josh 101

**Laura Washburn**
Brunch Quesadillas 38
Basic Grilled Cheese Sandwich 41
Mashed Potato Pie 109
Peach Cobbler 138

# PICTURE CREDITS

**Caroline Arber**
85, 95

**Martin Brigdale**
7, 33, 36–37, 50–51, 86,
108, 121, 128, 132–133,
136

**Peter Cassidy**
6T, 35, 54–55, 59–60,
62–63, 65–66, 83, 94,
96, 98, 103, 106–107,
114–116, 122–123

**Stephen Conroy**
28, 42, 47, 52–53, 111

**Laura Edwards**
134–135

**Tara Fisher**
11T, 34

**Jonathan Gregson**
56–57, 73

**Richard Jung**
93, 97, 101, 130

**Sandra Lane**
139

**Lisa Linder**
6B, 19–20

**William Lingwood**
21–23, 31, 45, 70–71,
72B, 75, 80–81, 82B, 90,
117–118

**James Merrell**
12T

**Gareth Morgans**
76–77, 79

**Getty Images/
Huw Jones**
49

**David Munns**
138

**Noel Murphy**
67

**Martin Norris**
74

**Steve Painter**
40, 89, 140

**William Reavell**
68, 127

**Debi Treloar**
p10, 1B, 13, 137

**Ian Wallace**
9T, 12B, 24, 30

**Philip Webb**
25, 27

**Isobel Wield**
38–39

**Kate Whitaker**
8, 14–17, 44, 58, 100,
112, 124–125

**Clare Winfield**
2, 104–105

**Polly Wreford**
26